THE COMPLETE ZODIAC ENTERTAINER

The Complete Zodiac Entertainer

Margaret M. Pearson

Cadbury Lamb

To Myriel and Elveda
with love

CONTENTS

INTRODUCTION

You are a good cook; everyone says so. You have a way with flowers, a gift for choosing presents. Mixing guests for your party is also one of the essential arts of being a good hostess. So is the wit to vary the type of party to suit your guest of honour, and to choose your other guests with thought to everyone's enjoyment.

Some people like impromptu cocktail parties; some more formal parties, with invitations issued well in advance. Some people prefer a theatre party; some like quiet parties; some like them gay and even noisy.

Not everyone responds with equal pleasure to the same colours, the same flowers, or even to the same sort of people. For instance, if your guest of honour is a Geminian, do not invite other Gemini people. They often dislike one another. On the other hand, if your principal guest is a Leo, ask some other Leos. They form a mutual admiration society!

So vary your parties to suit the personalities of your guests of honour; decorate your room with their favourite flowers; give them presents to suit their interests or their idiosyncrasies. Provide the right food and the right herbs for their sign, surround them with the right people *for them*—and every party will be a winner.

Aries

The Ram   21st March to 20th April

Giving a party for an Arien?

People born under this sign will prefer a large cocktail party to any other sort of entertainment, for they love a varied, gregarious life with plenty of good listeners about them while they expound the new schemes and original plans that are for ever buzzing in their heads.

YOUR GUESTS

To meet your Arien friends, ask some other Aries people—they get on well together—but spice the party with Ariens' usual best friends, creative Leos and quick-witted Sagittarians—admiring listeners for the Ariens' host of entertaining ideas, who can be relied on to keep their end up conversationally. Other people who mix well with Ariens are good-natured Librans, lively Geminians and Scorpios—full of electric vitality, and appreciative Capricorns who love amusing companions.

LUCKY DAYS

Lucky days for an Arien party are the first or ninth of the month, or a Tuesday.

ARIEN CHARACTERISTICS

Of course, you will not like all Ariens. But the ones you do like you find adventurous, energetic, kind, amusing, full of imagination, frank, optimistic, and possessing a contagious enthusiasm.

The ones you do not like (and therefore would not dream of entertaining) are self-centred, vain, aggressive, rude, domineering, quick-tempered, forgetful, rash, headstrong—and invariably late for appointments!

Ariens can be impulsive lovers, but they are often as fickle as weathercocks, so do not be swept off your feet if the end of your party is a trifle heady!

ICE-BREAKER

Few Aries people are shy, for their own schemes are always of first importance to them, and most of them can talk well on every subject under the sun, even if they know next to nothing about it. But some of the other guests may be less at ease, and one sure way to set everyone talking at a party is to mention 'fortunes'.

Ariens always want to know the future because they are always impatient for their new schemes to develop. Sometimes they themselves have quite a flair for reading cards. But it is unlucky to tell one's own future, so invite a guest who possesses this useful talent, or swot up a little fortune-telling yourself.

Give your guest of honour the cards to shuffle, spread them out fan-wise on a table, and let him choose thirteen cards (and make a silent wish). Deal these thirteen cards face upwards.

You need to remember only a few cards for this quick 'reading'. Your chief guest will have as his (or her) 'indicator' card the King or Queen of Diamonds (for a very fair, grey or white-haired person), Hearts (slightly less fair), Clubs (brown hair, brown eyes), or Spades (black hair, black eyes).

If your guest of honour's own 'indicator' card turns up in the thirteen, the answer to his unspoken wish is favourable, especially if the Nine of Hearts (the 'wish' card) is also there, or the Seven of Hearts (which indicates 'favours to come'). But be ready to comfort (or chaff) him if the Ace of Spades appears, for this indicates disappointment.

LUCKY STONES

If the party is a very special occasion, give your guest of honour a present embodying one of the Arien lucky stones—rubies, bloodstones, or garnets. Ariens' ruling planet is Mars, the 'red planet', so red stones of any kind give them a lift, and will bring them good hope, good health, and strength.

Rubies are a powerful amulet against poison, plague and sadness, and will protect the owner from enchantment by wicked spirits. He will be at peace with the world, secure and unafraid. Bloodstones bestow courage and tranquillity—and possess the magic to open all doors. According to Talmudic legend, a garnet supplied the only light in Noah's ark.

PRESENTS FOR ARIENS

Ariens often buy extravagant presents for themselves when they are in the money—even such an extravagance as a fast car. Both men and women are mechanically minded, so something for the car—a set of tools, perhaps —would be an ideal present. And as they are out-and-about people, give them a picnic set or barbecue equipment—or even a motoring map to help them find that ideal picnic spot. They also love team sports, so what about a photograph of their favourite football team, or a book on cricket?

They also like time-saving gadgets, such as an electric can-opener or food mixer, or a practical do-it-yourself present. But if you choose one of these sets, choose something that will not take too long to assemble. They are people who blow hot and blow cold, and their enthusiasm for some new project is likely to fade as suddenly as it erupted.

Both men and women can be demanding of their friends and hope, perhaps, for presents of expensive wrist-watches or furs, but they are also practical and sensible, and will be happy with a good diary and a new 'gadget' pencil. Arien girls also like snowy-white linen and lingerie.

(To please younger Ariens, give them a table tennis set, or a cricket bat. They love presents that involve physical activity.)

The lucky metal for Aries people is iron—so an orna-mental trivet would make a suitable present; or a hand-some wrought-iron antique key, to hang on the wall or to use as a paperweight.

LUCKY PERFUMES

If you would like to buy some scent for your Arien friend, choose musk, sandalwood, magnolia, jasmine or verbena.

LUCKY FLOWERS AND TREES

Every sign in the Zodiac has its own 'lucky' flowers and trees. For a party for an Arien, make your room bright with all the colours these people like—red, lively pinks, bronze-yellows, and orange.

Celandines, honeysuckle and daffodils are their lucky flowers. It was once thought that the juice of celandines improved eyes and in the Middle Ages the juice was dropped into the eyes of hawks and their owners—to make all of them 'hawk-eyed'. Honeysuckle denotes generous and devoted affection. Daffodils are said to cover the Elysian Fields—the 'Paradise' of the ancient Greeks.

Ariens' lucky trees are hawthorns—but remember hawthorns are holy trees for both Christians and pagans. The Crown of Thorns was made of hawthorns, so the tree became endowed with power against satanic spirits and ghosts. In ancient Greece, hawthorn was used as a marriage torch, and girls were given crowns of hawthorn at their weddings. Sprigs of hawthorn were considered to have miraculous powers against storms at sea. Hawthorns are also associated with the fairies, so never cut a branch of hawthorn—even for an Arien party—without first asking the fairies' permission.

Ariens seem particularly vulnerable to evil spirits as well as to ill-intentioned fairies, so hang an onion in the house to keep witches away, and give them a sprig of rosemary to wear as a protection against black magic and lightning.

There are many legends about rosemary. During the Flight into Egypt, the Virgin Mary spread her cloak on a rosemary bush to dry. The previously white flowers immediately turned blue. 'Rosemary for remembrance' refers to the old belief that the constant use of rosemary tisanes (or tea) would improve a bad memory. The Greeks wore wreaths of rosemary when sitting for exams. Like lavender, rosemary is said to grow more fragrantly in Britain than elsewhere. Sir Thomas More allowed it to grow all over his garden in Chelsea because it was an emblem of loyal friendship (though it did not prove so to him, so far as Henry VIII was concerned). There is also an old proverb about rosemary: 'Where rosemary grows, Missus is Master.'

HERBS AND FOODS

Various herbs and foods are specially beneficial to people born under the different Zodiac signs. There is a good selection for Aries people, who both eat well and cook well, and who like both flavour and colour in their food.

Ariens should eat onions and rosemary as well as having them nearby. Rosemary tea will be good for their headaches, and essence of rosemary will give their hair beauty and sheen.

Many herbs besides rosemary are good for Ariens—horseradish, mustard, pepper, marjoram and garlic.

Horseradish has been cultivated for the medicinal properties of its roots since very early times. It was used as a stimulant, an antiseptic, and as a treatment for paralysis, rheumatism, epilepsy—and toothache.

The ancient Greeks recommended mustard seeds as an antidote for the bite of a scorpion, to draw out splinters and to strengthen the heart.

Pepper was once almost priceless—so precious that the berries were counted out one by one. Centuries before Christ, pepper was a staple commodity of trade, and was often demanded in payment of taxes. It was in such demand by the wealthy that land was often leased in return for a fixed quantity of pepper. The term 'a pepper-corn rent' has survived to this day. Now it means a purely nominal rent, but in medieval times it must often have been a heavy burden to tenants.

Marjoram was once planted on graves—to charm the souls of the loved ones. Ancient Greek physicians prescribed it for poisoning and dropsy, and recommended its use as a fomentation. A handful of fresh tops infused in a pint of boiling water often helps to relieve nervous headaches.

Garlic was once regarded as a 'heal-all', to cure everything from whooping cough and toothache to rheumatism and freckles. It was also an aid to digestion, an antiseptic and a disinfectant. Medieval doctors, when visiting their patients, often carried a clove of garlic as a combined charm and a disinfectant. Louis XIV's doctor, Monsieur de L'Orme, went one better. He always kept a piece of garlic in his mouth and stuck a piece of rue in each nostril. He may have looked and smelled peculiar, but it kept him healthy and he lived to be ninety-four. Garlic was one of the chief items in the diet of Egyptian slaves and labourers, who enjoyed it as a food and valued it as a medicine and for its magical properties. In those days, 15lb of garlic would buy a healthy slave, and cocks (and soldiers) fed on garlic were regarded as 'the most stout to fight'. Garlic was probably introduced to Europe by Crusaders. It is still used in superstitious eastern Europe to rub on window-frames and doorknobs to discourage vampires, witches, warlocks and werewolves.

For fruit, Ariens should eat blackberries, rhubarb, citrus fruit, apples, dates, olives, raspberries and figs. (Olives, olive oil, figs, almonds, garlic, goat cheese and honey were in all probability the staple diet of Christ and the apostles.)

For vegetables, Ariens should eat not only onions, but also tomatoes, celery, potatoes, cabbage and spinach.

And as Ariens are impatient people, have everything ready to begin the party the moment the guest of honour rings the doorbell!

Taurus

The Bull   21st April to 21st May

Giving a party for a Taurean?

Taureans love parties and are excellent and appreciative guests who will be ready to compliment you warmly and thank you sincerely. But their standards are high—so put out your best silver, use your best tablecloth, buy the best food you can afford, cook it to the best of your ability, and serve it not only with good wine but with some little personal, preferably romantic touch, such as a rose by your chief guest's side plate.

Taureans would put themselves out for *you;* they will expect *you* to put yourself out for *them*.

Taureans like a well-planned life—and something to look forward to—so issue your invitations well in advance. As they are rather formal people, plan a formal dinner party, but as they are also romantic, have soft lights, beautiful flower arrangements and soft music in the background.

YOUR GUESTS

To meet your Taurean friend, invite some Leos and Sagittarians, who share their love of good food and wine. But also ask some guests from their 'best friend' groups—Scorpios (who are also in the gourmet class), Virgoans (like Taureans, discriminating, with excellent taste), and Aquarians (original people, who may turn up at the party with a beautifully wrapped present no one else would have thought of).

Hold the party on the sixth of the month, or on a Friday, the lucky day for Taureans.

TAUREAN CHARACTERISTICS

The Taureans you like have a great sense of beauty, are charming and considerate guests, practical, genuine, full of common sense, sympathetic, loyal and affectionate. They have excellent taste in dress, interior decoration, food and wine—and often have pleasing singing voices.

Taureans you do not like are envious, obstinate, frivolous, *too* fond of their creature comforts, dull, plodding, and too conservative, and if they do not agree with you, they will raise their voices and talk you into submission—or revolt.

ICE-BREAKER

Legend says that Noah left the ark on 29th April—a Taurean date. So try your hand at a really original party piece. Bake your favourite plain cake, ice it, and decorate it with chocolate zoological creatures. Lindt's and Suchard's manufacture packets of chocolate creatures— little bears, for instance, and butterflies—and with a modicum of ingenuity, you could create a 'Noah's ark cake' that would really set your guests laughing.

While they are enjoying the cake, entertain your guests with 'The Luck of the Aces'. A Heart means a love letter. A Diamond means courtship. A Club means good luck in business. A Spade means a meeting with a loved one. The aces, if reversed, indicate disappointment, a threatened loss, a delayed letter or sickness.

Discard all the sixes and under, leaving thirty-two cards. Shuffle and deal thirteen. If an ace appears, put it aside. Shuffle again, deal again. This should be done three times only. The earlier the aces appear, the better the luck. An Ace of Spades, however, is never entirely lucky, and if turned up first, it can still mean tears, or a parting, or that patience is needed before your guest's hope will come true.

LUCKY STONES

A present embodying one of their lucky stones will enchant any Taurean guest of honour. The principal ones are emeralds, turquoises or red coral.

Emeralds are a good aid for memory and bring success in love. Turquoise gives courage to the wearer, and prevents quarrels between man and wife. Red coral is a protection against epilepsy and the Evil Eye. From very ancient times, red coral has been used in charms and amulets. It was once thought to turn pale if the owner were ill, regaining its true colour as he regained his strength.

Taureans' ruling planet is Venus, whose colour is blue. To bring true harmony to their lives, blue should be the predominating colour in their surroundings. Blue is the colour denoting affection—and Taureans can inspire great love and devotion. Pink and rose also bring them happiness—but never introduce red. Remember the old tag, 'like a red rag to a bull'.

PRESENTS FOR TAUREANS

Taurus people of all ages can be obstinate—even mulish—but they will usually melt under the influence of quiet music and soft colours, so a record-player beautifully wrapped would make a fine present. (At all costs, avoid a noisy present and discordant colours. They upset Taureans.)

Home decorating and flower arranging are often

Taurean hobbies. They have an innate artistic flair, and usually create a comfortable background for themselves, rich in colour and with beautiful ornaments. Those interests give good clues for presents.

Taureans are enchanted by rich textures—velvets, silks, and soft woollies. Silk shirts will be appreciated by Taurean men. All of them love good living, and are artists at relaxing, and as they love long hot baths, give them scented bath oils and expensive soap, and a paperback to read while they lie back in heaven-scented luxury. They will also appreciate a bottle of wine, a home winemaking kit, or some exotic food.

Taurean girls are delightfully feminine, and take great interest in their personal appearance, and love expensive jewellery (especially necklaces) and expensive scent. But though Taureans are luxury lovers, they are immensely practical—thrifty and clever shoppers and skilful with their hands. Taurean women often make their own clothes, so any sewing accessory would be a welcome present. Taureans enjoy games involving their hands or words, so consider Scrabble or a book of crossword puzzles.

Taureans also like gifts of money and, being good shoppers, they can be trusted to buy something that will be a compliment to your good taste. (Taurus boys like construction sets, girls jewellery kits or mini sewing machines—*mini*, not *toy*, however. Even as children, Taureans are practical, and prefer their presents to be practical.)

Taureans' lucky metal is copper, and their pleasure in good craftsmanship will guarantee appreciation of a copper kettle, an old warming pan, or copper cooking utensils.

LUCKY PERFUMES

Softly sensuous perfumes are right for Taureans, such as rose, carnation, gardenia, lily of the valley and lilac.

LUCKY FLOWERS AND TREES

When entertaining a Taurean friend, decorate your room as beautifully as you can. Their lucky flowers include some simple favourites, cowslips (whose scent calms the heart and strengthens the brain), violets, and daisies (once, long ago, called the 'day's eye'). And just for fun, if you can find any, have a spectacularly big bowl of foxgloves, a fairy plant.

There are countless legends concerning roses. One says that the Archangel Gabriel twisted 150 roses into wreaths for the Virgin Mary—a red wreath to symbolise her sorrows, a white wreath for her gladness, and a wreath of golden roses to symbolise her glory. Roses once had great religious significance, and early 'rosaries' were made of pounded rose petals moulded into beads, giving off a sweet scent when held in warm hands.

In the old days a rose was carved or painted on the ceiling of a chamber or banqueting hall, or people wore chaplets of roses, if the proceedings were to be kept *sub rosa*, meaning 'under the rose' or 'secret'. The custom was based on the story of how Cupid, the son of Venus, gave a rose to Harpocrates, the god of silence, to bribe him not to disclose the indiscretions of Venus on her amorous adventures.

Violets were once widely used in medicine, in love philtres and syrups, to flavour puddings, and to make wine. Violets were once a symbol of innocence, and were worn as garlands on all festive occasions.

If it is not the right time of the year for flowers, trails of ivy will bring luck around the house to Taurean women, and sprigs of holly will bring luck to a Taurean man. Being an evergreen, and having red berries, holly has always been regarded as a symbol of everlasting life, and consequently as a lucky plant.

HERBS AND FOODS

The best herbs for Taureans are thyme, mint and the almost forgotten tansy.

The delicate fragrance of thyme was so popular among the ancient Greeks that to be told one smelt of thyme was considered an agreeable compliment. This herb was brought to Britain by the Romans who used it medicinally, in thyme vinegar to relieve headaches, and in an ointment to relieve the pain of gout and rheumatism. A sprig of thyme under your pillow is said to prevent nightmares.

Mint was also brought to Britain by the Romans and was always one of the herbs cultivated in monastery gardens. It was prescribed for bee-stings, bruises and headaches. Present-day herbalists say that mint tea strengthens weak stomachs.

Tansy was once found in every cottage garden, and was widely used in puddings and cakes. Most people today find tansy too strong and gingery, but tansy pudding is still a traditional Easter pudding in some parts of England, the leaves being used for the flavouring. Tansy was once eaten to help counteract the effect of eating too-heavy winter foods and too much salt fish.

For fruit, give Taureans blackberries, cherries, gooseberries, pears, plums, strawberries and peaches. The branches of peach-trees are said to be a very powerful protection against witches and the Devil and even a carving of a peach over a door will keep demons away.

For vegetables, serve beans, lentils, potatoes, peas and

carrots, beetroot, leeks and onions, tomatoes and celeriac.

When you are relaxing with your coffee, serve one of the liqueurs made from the various Taurean fruits, such as cherry brandy, peach brandy, slivovitz, the plum brandy from Yugoslavia—or, of course, the liqueur that is specially suited for Taureans, crème de menthe, the mint-flavoured liqueur.

Gemini

The Twins   22nd May to 21st June

Giving a party for a Geminian?

A cheerful, gay, and even noisy wine and cheese party (with plenty of substantial and unusual sandwiches to keep up their boundless energy) would be just right for a Geminian. Mulled wine is an excellent party drink in the winter. For warmer days, serve iced wine punch garnished with a fruity, floating ice ring into which are set cherries, rose petals, mint leaves, and violets. Your guest of honour will be enchanted at its prettiness and at your originality.

Be as dashing as possible with your sandwiches—have them large, small, hot, chilled, round and square. Use white bread, brown, brown and white together, rye bread —even muffins.

YOUR GUESTS

Gemini people like sparkling conversation on a great variety of subjects with stimulating companions. They love (and need) companionship, and, owing to the duality of their nature, they usually have two distinct interests flourishing at the same time.

So, to meet your Geminian friend, ask some lively-minded Leos, some Aquarians (who usually share some interest with a Geminian), some cheerful and intuitive Sagittarians, and some Librans. Librans are often psychic, and have a strange affinity with nature. These qualities intrigue Geminians, and help to keep the party conversation spread over a wide field, and *that* always stimulates a Geminian. (Do not, however, ask other Gemini guests. They often dislike one another.)

LUCKY DAYS

Hold the party on the fifth of the month, or on a Wednesday—their lucky days.

GEMINIAN CHARACTERISTICS

Of course, nobody likes everybody, but the Geminians you like are charming, good guests (and good hosts), are interested in a dozen different things, and can talk well about all of them. They are cheerful, generous, thoughtful, artistic, quick-witted, tactful, versatile, and engagingly full of enthusiasms.

The ones you do not like—and would avoid at all costs —are superficial, inconsistent, restless, too effusive, over-ambitious for social position, and self-indulgent, and their talent for talk can turn them into 'con men'—or bores.

As to their love life, remember that Geminians like to have two irons in every fire, and are not always *quite* sincere in their declarations of undying affection!

ICE-BREAKER

A part of the duality of many Gemini people is that they have the gift of second sight. Even if they do not possess this gift, they are intrigued with astrology, fortune-telling, palmistry—and with luck foretold by the throw of the dice. So all you need to set your party going is to provide three dice, and to learn what the different numbers mean. The dice can be rattled in a glass.

Say your chief guest throws a 3, 5 and 6. Add them together $(3+5+6=14; 1+4=5)$. Remember what you have learnt about number 5, and tell your guest that an important newcomer is going to cross her path. The 'message of the dice' can be elaborated by also giving the meaning of the other numbers—3 and 6. Number 3 brings promise of an unexpected gift (from the important newcomer?), while number 6 brings a warning of the loss of something of value. So a quick-witted hostess could easily make these ingredients into an entertaining prediction!

'Divination by Dice' is an age-old custom. The numbers that can be scored by throwing three dice at a time vary from 3 to 18. Double figures can be read as they stand, and also when reduced by addition to a single figure. So if 18 is thrown, take 9 (1 + 8) into account as well as the three 6s, and remember that three of a kind deliver the message more strongly than two of a kind, and much more strongly than a single number.

Here are the 'Divinations of the Dice' to learn before your party:

3. A pleasant surprise amid good influences.
4. You are hedged about with worry but the clouds are already beginning to pass.
5. An important newcomer is going to cross your path.
6. A happy throw—indicating good luck, and an engagement or wedding in the offing.
7. Guard your tongue, and do not believe all you hear.
8. Trouble—and it's your own fault.
9. Guard your money and your jewellery. You are in danger of losing something of value.
10. You will hear of a birth, and be asked to a party.
11. A friend's quarrel or illness will affect you.
12. Important news is coming to your home.
13. You will say goodbye to a lover or a close friend.
14. Happiness surrounds you, and a secret wish comes true.

15. Keep your own counsel, and don't become involved in other people's problems.
16. A journey or a new job—something to celebrate.
17. Good fortune or an unexpected invitation through someone older than yourself.
18. An excellent throw—'good luck' three times over. Everything will go well with you, and you will achieve promotion, friendship, love and happiness.

LUCKY STONES

If your guest of honour is a very special friend, give her a present embodying one of the Geminian lucky stones— sapphires (a magical stone, preserving innocence, promoting chaste thoughts and improving the wearer's manners!), diamonds (the 'king' of gems), or agates (an antidote to the poison of spiders and scorpions). If you are buying one of the lucky stones for a Gemini girlfriend, choose a setting of great delicacy. She may be tall—even statuesque—but she loves the daintiest of jewellery.

Geminians' ruling planet is Mercury, whose colours are silvery white and iridescent pale blue. So decorate your room in these colours (silvered fronds of fern or a silver Christmas tree would appeal specially to these guests)—and have clusters of tall candles to cast the shimmering light which delights Geminians.

Ferns, by the way, protect a house from thunder and lightning.

PRESENTS FOR GEMINIANS

Restless Geminians love to travel, so look for presents that will make travelling smoother—a travelling iron, electric hair rollers, compact makeup kits, pens, writing cases and suitcases. If the presents are a bit gimmicky, so much the better.

They often have a strong competitive streak, and enjoy puzzles. Some of them are very good with their hands, and would appreciate a well fitted-out sewing box, or a set of tools. They like to impress people, so give them *big* books. 'Coffee table' books are a joy to these people— about practically anything, as Geminians will be interested in almost everything from golf to foreign languages, at some time in their lives. (They are often bilingual. Gemini people never like just one of anything.) They would also be intrigued by some offbeat, well-produced encyclopaedia.

Most Geminians are gregarious—happiest in company —so a present that will involve others is a good buy for them—a punch bowl and matching goblets, or a set of tarot cards, or lovely table mats and napkins for the dinner parties they excel at arranging. They have crowds of friends, so they constantly need new address books and birthday books.

(Group games and puzzles make the best presents for young Gemini friends. They are live-wire youngsters, always on the go, and they have a competitive spirit that can be catered for with well thought-out presents.)

Geminians' chief lucky metal is silver, which gives you great scope for presents, from a cigarette box or a silver thimble to silver earrings. Or, as quicksilver (or mercury) is also lucky for these people, buy them a barometer!

LUCKY PERFUMES

Scents to please a Gemini friend are lavender, lilac, sweet pea, honeysuckle, mignonette and gardenia.

LUCKY FLOWERS AND TREES

Lavender, maidenhair fern and lily of the valley are lucky plants for Gemini people.

Lavender leaves and flower buds make a fragrant and

relaxing tea—even more comforting if drunk when wearing a nightcap with lavender quilted into it!

Lilies of the valley were once known as 'Our Lady's tears'; tradition says they first sprang up where her tears fell to the ground under the Cross. A drug made from every part of the plant was used as a heart medicine—and to improve the memory.

Myrtle is also lucky for Geminians. It was once associated with love and marriage, and was woven into bridal wreaths until orange blossom superseded it in popularity. Like rosemary and parsley, myrtle is said to grow best for women.

HERBS AND FOODS

Various herbs and foods specially beneficial to Geminians include parsley. It is rich in vitamins A, B and C, and it is a waste to use it only as a garnish. *Eat* it! It does everyone good. Parsley came into popularity as a garnish in the Middle Ages, when guests often suspected the intentions of their hosts when invited to dine. As parsley was regarded as an antidote to poison, to place it on a dish was taken as a sign of good faith.

Another good herb for Geminians is vervain, once as highly venerated by the Druids as mistletoe. Christians regarded it as a holy plant, as it was discovered growing under the Cross at Calvary. So it was valued as a protection against evil—and no witch would enter a house where a sprig of vervain was hanging.

Two other Geminian herbs are caraway and liquorice. Caraway was much used in ancient times for medicinal purposes, and was a popular ingredient in love potions. As for liquorice, it has long been used to disguise the taste of medicines, and to flavour sweets and tobacco.

For fruit, give Gemini people oranges, lemons, grapefruit, peaches, plums, pineapple, apricots, figs and dates (both of which were once regarded as holy trees), and mulberries. As mulberries have always been cultivated extensively for the culture of silkworms, a mulberry is looked upon as a symbol of industry.

For vegetables, all the following are good for Geminians: tomatoes, celery, beans, sprouts, mushrooms, carrots, sweet corn, parsnips, watercress, lettuce, asparagus and cauliflower.

If you are serving coffee and liqueurs at the end of your party, there are some liqueurs that will appeal specially to your Gemini guests. These are anisette; curaçao, grand marnier and vanderhum (all made from citrus fruit); apricot brandy—and especially kümmel, the German liqueur, containing oil of caraway.

Cancer

The Crab   22nd June to 21st July

Giving a party for a Cancerian?

People born under this sign make rewarding guests, because they respond so readily to any display of affection —because they so thoroughly enjoy parties—and because they enjoy being the centre of attraction.

They also like trying out new dishes, and will appreciate anything out of the ordinary (well-cooked!) that you like to serve. They love little surprises and unexpected gifts, and enjoy a well-set table, a friendly setting, and the glow of a fire on a winter's night. They like an informal party, with plenty of room (and time) to 'circulate' and talk to old friends and new.

Tell them the tradition behind any of the foods you serve. It is unlucky, for instance, to put bread on the table upside down, because that encourages the Devil to fly over the house. Bread has often been regarded as sacred, either symbolically or in itself. There is a sensible Spanish proverb which says: 'All sorrows are less with bread.'

Your Cancerian guest will listen to these stories intently, at the same time taking in every detail of the setting—the colours, the lighting, the flowers. And while listening, your guest will be quietly summing up the characters of the other guests, and quite likely will give you accurate word pictures of them later on.

YOUR GUESTS

To meet your Cancerian friend, ask some other Cancerians (they understand each other's ups and downs), some Pisceans (often as mystical as Cancerians), Scorpios (entertaining guests, with their talent for telling a good story), a few of the intuitive Aquarians, some practical Taureans and Capricorns (who appeal to the practical side of Cancerians), and some romantic Virgoans.

LUCKY DAYS

The luckiest days to hold your Cancerian party are the second or third of the month, or a Monday.

CANCERIAN CHARACTERISTICS

For your party, invite the Cancerians you find kind, courteous, understanding, romantic, affectionate, hardworking, sociable, protective, good home-makers—and good money-makers.

Leave off your list the Cancerians you find distrustful, stubborn, possessive, too withdrawn, cynical, quick to take offence, humourless and disloyal.

In their love life, Cancerians are both placid and emotional. Their emotion is easily roused, and all their lives they daydream of adventure and romance. If the world presses around them, they escape into a world of their own. They need intervals of comparative solitude, so if they go off into a corner quietly by themselves during your party, don't think it odd. Just leave them alone to get on with it!

ICE-BREAKER

Cancerians are often psychic, so show them what *you* can do in a game of 'character reading' for six guests at a time.

Take the King, Queen and Jack of Diamonds, and the Ace, Two and Three of Hearts. Add twenty-one other cards at random, thus making twenty-seven altogether—a multiple of the mystic number nine.

Shuffle the cards well, and let the guests draw one each. Those who do not draw one of the special cards can try again later, but those who do draw one should rest on their laurels and withdraw from the game!

Here is the meaning of the six 'character reading' cards:

The *King of Diamonds* denotes a lover of pleasure—of good food and wine.

The *Queen of Diamonds* has many friends, and will hold an important position in the public eye.

The *Jack of Diamonds* is a cheerful person, full of fun and frivolity, and self-confidence.

The *Ace of Hearts* denotes a lazy person, but one who has considerable ability. Latent ambition here needs a prod!

The *Two of Hearts* indicates a generous man but a 'close' woman. Ask him for a loan, but never her. But you can ask her for advice, for though she is 'close' with money, she can be a wise counsellor.

The *Three of Hearts* brings a warning of disappointments and delays; whoever draws this card needs a cheer-up drink, quickly!

LUCKY STONES

As a special gift for a special Cancerian guest, choose a present embodying one of their lucky stones—carnelians (a protection against collapsing houses), sapphires (the enemy of anger), diamonds (which signify sincerity and constancy, and prevent the approach of old age), and emeralds (their chief mascot, and a good aid for the memory).

Cancerians' ruling planet is the moon, whose colours are green, mauve, white and silvery grey.

PRESENTS FOR CANCERIANS

Tradition, home and family are all of great importance to Cancerians, and anything that adds to the comfort and beauty of their background would be a suitable gift. Cancer women are often excellent cooks, and would welcome books on entertaining and hostess cooking—or herbs, or frames for photographs of their families. But they do not like housework, so give them a scarf, in chiffon or silk, in the sea-greeny colours they love, or exquisite handkerchiefs rather than an apron

For Cancer men (most of whom love the sea) nothing could be better than books on a subject combining tradition and the sea, such as the development of the navy—or explorations by sea. They all seem to be great collectors— of coins, perhaps, so give them books on numismatics—or just give them books, so long as they are about the sea, or history, or antiques, or the origin of their own family. Swimming togs, water-skiing equipment, or something for their humble dinghy or their fabulous yacht would also be excellent presents.

Cancerians also like gifts for the home, and will sentimentally treasure presents that celebrate a special occasion. House plants are also good presents. Cancerians have green fingers.

(Young Cancerians have a grown-up interest in collecting, and additions to a stamp or coin collection would make good presents for boys. Girls often collect dolls, and both boys and girls like books.)

The lucky metal for Cancerians is silver, so the choice

of appropriate presents is endless, from an elegant tea-spoon to an antique silver treasure (preferably with some 'story' attached to it).

LUCKY PERFUMES

Scents to give Cancerians are violet, lily of the valley, lilac, white rose, Californian poppy, and honeysuckle.

LUCKY FLOWERS AND TREES

Green is a tricky colour for mortals to dabble with. It is the favourite colour of the fairies, and they are said to resent humans wearing it. So do not *wear* green for your Cancerian party, but use it without hesitation in decorating your home along with the Cancerians' lucky flowers—roses, poppies, and wallflowers.

Roses are old, old flowers, and the rose garden of King Midas was one of the wonders of the ancient world. Confucius mentioned the rose gardens of Peking. In the twelfth century the English enjoyed an exotic rose-petal liqueur, and rose syrup was a staple of medieval pharmacies. The origin of the phrase, 'a bed of roses', refers to the Sybarites, who slept on beds filled with petals. (Sybaris was a Greek city in ancient Italy, famous for its luxurious way of life.) Rose petals can be used most beautifully, frozen separately in ice cubes to float in drinks of rosé wine.

Legend has always regarded poppies as the flower of sleep and oblivion, and they were once used in both magic and medicine to calm the passions of love.

Like roses, wallflowers are very old flowers. They were grown in most monastery gardens, as oil of wallflowers was once believed to cure boils and eye complaints. As wallflowers will grow almost anywhere—including cracks in stone walls—they were once affectionately known as 'the solace of prisoners'.

HERBS AND FOODS

Herbs particularly beneficial to Cancerians are valerian, chives and poppy seeds.

Valerian was a popular ingredient in love philtres. It was also prescribed for nervous disorders, rickets, insomnia and coughs. The Greeks used it to arrest bleeding. A valerian tisane is still recommended by herbalists as a tranquilliser. The smell of valerian roots sends cats and rats into ecstasies—and it was probably valerian roots that enticed the rats to follow the Pied Piper rather than the magic music of his flute.

Chives are a universally popular herb, known all over the world long before the Christian era. Countless pairs of scissors still snip chives into cottage cheese, shrimp cocktails, omelettes, and stuffings.

Poppy seeds have a high fat content, and they were popular with Greeks and Romans, who ate them with honey and wine. In Nero's time one of the great delicacies was stuffed roasted dormice spread with honey and rolled in poppy seeds!

For fruit, give Cancerians plenty of fresh fruit of all kinds, especially oranges and prunes stewed with honey. For vegetables, serve cucumber, red cabbage, kale, watercress, pumpkin, onions and lettuce. (Both wild and cultivated, lettuce is said to have the power of arousing love and preventing intoxication.) Cancerians should also drink plenty of milk, and eat cottage cheese, cream cheese, and raisins.

With the coffee, serve one of the liqueurs made with a citrus fruit base, such as strega, the orange-flavoured Italian liqueur, or curaçao, or grand marnier (flavoured with orange peel), or vanderhum (flavoured with tangerines).

Jupiter is said to have given Juno an orange at their wedding, and that is why orange blossom is so popular as a bridal flower. Orange blossom was introduced into Europe by the Crusaders. It was regarded as the symbol of purity, chastity and eternal love. Oranges were used by witches in various malefic ceremonies—for instance, as the symbol of a victim's heart when plotting mischief. The victim's name was written on a piece of paper, stuck to the orange with pins—and thrust up the chimney till the victim sickened or died.

Before the guests begin looking for their coats, tell them about strega, the lovely golden liqueur commonly called 'witches' brew'. It is too good to leave to witches, for legend says that when two people share a strega, they are united 'by a love that lasts for ever'. How better to end a party than to share a strega with another guest?

Leo

The Lion   22nd July to 23rd August

Giving a party for a Leo?

People born under this sign make some of the most satisfactory and rewarding guests, as they are sociable, more than keep their end up conversationally, appreciate gourmet standards in food and wine—and just enjoy parties!

Don't aim at too formal a party, and allow plenty of time, as Leos are born entertainers and can keep everyone amused with a string of anecdotes. But they like their talents to be appreciated, and will not like their audience snatched away from them for no good reason!

YOUR GUESTS

To meet your Leo friends, ask some Ariens (as long as they have strong personalities), some other Leos (they appreciate each other's generosity and independence), some Aquarians (who applaud Leos' creative ability), some cool, clever and artistic Taureans, and some Sagittarians, whose occasional moods of 'careless abandon' appeal to the flamboyant, dashing streak in so many Leos.

LUCKY DAYS

Hold your Leo party on the first or the fourth of the month, or on a Sunday.

LEO CHARACTERISTICS

Some people consider Leos to be 'show-offs' because

they love to be the centre of attraction. But when you like them you will find them generous, affectionate, loyal, intuitive, excellent organisers, good actors, kind, courageous, and full of fun and enthusiasm.

The Leos you do not like are the ones you find overbearing, egotistical, arrogant, lazy, proud, too vain, too gregarious, too ambitious, extravagant, too easily swayed by flattery, and too demanding of constant admiration.

As to their love life, Leos are romantic and chivalrous, and may well arrive with all the trimmings, including flowers . . . and soft words. But many Leos are better actors than they (or you) may realise, and at times they become carried away by their own dramatic skill. So don't, on the night of your party, accept a proposal as impulsively as it may be offered.

ICE-BREAKER

All Leo people love an audience, and they love to talk about their gardens, even if it is window-box gardening.

Many leaders, including Napoleon, were born under the sign of Leo, and this side of their character is usually emphasised in horoscopes, but as they are the most green-fingered sign, enthuse about your guest of honour's garden and tell him about the favourite flowers of some famous people.

Napoleon's own favourite flower was the violet. He first met Josephine de Beauharnais at a ball where she was wearing a coronet and carrying a bouquet of violets, which she later threw to him from her carriage. In memory of this romantic first meeting, Napoleon always sent her violets on their wedding anniversaries. Violets became the emblem of the Bonapartists as Napoleon, banished to Elba, said defiantly, 'I shall return in the spring . . . with the violets!'

Josephine herself loved roses above all other flowers, and the development of the rose owes much to the enthusiasm and lavish sums of money she devoted to her garden at Malmaison. She also paid Redouté a salary of 18,000 francs a year to paint her roses for her.

The favourite flowers of Queen Elizabeth I were germander speedwell, heartsease, the wild strawberry flower, and carnations.

Germander speedwell (with its bright blue flowers) was once regarded as an emblem of truth and friendship. In some places in England it was known as 'remember me' and 'wish me well'. 'Speed well!' was an old form of leave-taking.

Heartsease is a name given today to a wild pansy, but in Elizabeth's time the name was given to wallflowers. In those days everyone understood the language of flowers, and Elizabeth would have appreciated the significance of the wallflower—'fidelity in adversity'.

The wild strawberry she might have seen almost anywhere in her 'progresses' through her kingdom, for this little pure white 'rose' with its trefoil leaves and shining red fruit flourishes on shady banks and in woodland clearings.

The old name for a carnation was gillyflower, a corruption of the Latin word *caryophyllum*, which means a clove. These carnations were probably what we know today as 'pinks'. In the seventeenth and eighteenth centuries their petals were used as a substitute for the expensive Indian cloves to spice wines and ales and to flavour cordials, syrups and vinegars. At one time the wearing of a carnation meant that the wearer was betrothed, and that other suitors could give up their pursuit.

Your Leo guest will have some story of his own to

tell—he always has—so give him his head. You will find out a lot about flowers that you did not know before.

LUCKY STONES

A special present for a special guest should embody one of the Leo lucky stones—gold, chrysolite and amber.

As gold does not rust, it was regarded by the old physicians as possessing curative properties, and they made up ointments containing gold leaf to revitalise the aged.

Astrologers wore charms of chrysolite as a protection against evil, nightmares and melancholy; these also endowed the wearer with occult powers.

Amber is one of the oldest mascots in the world. To the Chinese, amber embodied the soul of a tiger, so it became a symbol of courage. Ancient physicians regarded amber beads as a cure for fever and goitre, and a talisman against all kinds of danger. Powdered amber, mixed with honey and oil of roses, was prescribed for earache.

Leo's ruling planet is the sun, and the lucky colours for people born under this sign are gold, all shades of yellow, cream, warm orange—and pale green.

PRESENTS FOR LEOS

Leo people always feel they are someone special. And they often *are* someone special. So they like personalised gifts, such as gold cuff-links, or a real leather wallet, or a sealing-wax stamp incorporating their initials—or personalised notepaper, or car accessories, name-stamped books of matches—practically anything so long as it is handsome, and obviously belongs to *him*.

Women Leos are the same. They like their presents to be expensive, and personalised. They like gold charms, a gold amulet or watch, or beautiful, initialled handkerchiefs. They are very feminine creatures. They love frilly undies, heady scent, luxurious chocolates, scented soap, expensive seats at the opera, rings and baubles, something elegant and extravagant for the house—or one long-stemmed yellow rose

Antiques appeal to all Leos, so books on collecting antiques would make good gifts. And as Leos are the most green-fingered people in the Zodiac, give them plants for their garden or pot plants for their flat, or books on gardening, or Redouté prints of yellow roses.

Leo men are often inspired 'Mr Fix-its', coping with anything from frozen pipes to a broken toy train. So a set of tools would make an excellent present. As a surprise present, give your Leos a photograph of themselves. (They are vain people; they will love it.)

(Leo children are often high-spirited—sometimes rather too much so—so choose presents that will use up some of this surplus energy, such as a football, a bicycle, or a skipping rope. They love parties more than most children, and love dressing up, for they seem to be born with the idea that all the world's *their* stage.)

Gold is the metal for this royal sign of the Zodiac.

Leos *love* presents—golden presents—so do your best!

LUCKY PERFUMES

Leos like heady perfumes such as orange blossom, heliotrope, red rose, sandalwood or verbena.

LUCKY FLOWERS AND TREES

Nearly all yellow and orange flowers are lucky for Leos, as they are considered to reflect the sun. Marigolds (which symbolise constancy and endurance in love) are particularly lucky. A marigold ointment is soothing for ulcers, wounds, and bee-stings. In America, there is a legend that marigolds sprang from the blood of those slain during

Hernando Cortes' conquest of Mexico in the sixteenth century.

Marigolds, sunflowers, light-coloured peonies and yellow roses will evoke a warm response if banked into a floral arrangement for your Leo guest. Sunflowers originated in Peru. After their introduction into England, the English decided that sunflower seeds soaked in whisky were good for rheumatism.

Peonies have been venerated as a magical and healing plant for thousands of years. Pythagoras recommended the wearing of a necklet of peony seeds to prevent epilepsy, and both seeds and roots were incorporated into charms against witches or to dispel storms and secure release from enchantment.

HERBS AND FOODS

For Leos, the best herbs are angelica, rue, fennel, pepper and parsley.

Angelica received its name because an archangel—St Michael—personally revealed its power as a cure for the plague. It was also esteemed as a protection against witches and spells, while chewing angelica root was regarded as a cure for almost any trouble. As the roots yield an oil that flavours various liqueurs, such as chartreuse, there was probably something in the belief that chewing the roots would bring comfort.

Rue was a magical herb, to ward off goblins, and the Romans, who brought it to England, believed it had the power to bestow second sight—and to cure toadstool poisoning. The grey leaves of rue are said to have been the model for the Clubs on playing-cards.

Fennel has been used for centuries by physicians, who prescribed it for eye ailments, while everyone stuffed it into keyholes to keep out ghosts.

Most Leos like spicy foods, and are adventurous eaters, very willing to try something new, provided they know it will be well cooked. Leos should eat cabbage, peppers, grapes, eggs, oranges and lemons, plums, peas, lettuce, asparagus, coconut, nuts and raisins.

Black coffee, a bowl of nuts and raisins, and a glass of chartreuse will finish the party with a flourish.

Virgo

The Virgin   24th August to 22nd September

Giving a party for a Virgoan?

People born under this sign love luxury, and are perfectionists to their well-manicured fingertips, but they are also realists, and know that if they do not accept invitations from anyone less than a millionaire, they are not likely to go to many parties.

So they will be delighted to accept an invitation to your party. Though reserved, Virgo people are warm and affectionate, but being reserved, they will appreciate seeing some familiar faces when they open your door and walk in.

So do not throw them into a group composed entirely of strangers. That would be unkind to Virgoans, who blossom slowly—but graciously—when surrounded by the approval of friends.

Virgo people like the opposite sex. So if you are having a small dinner party, watch while you serve the pre-dinner drinks. See who your Virgoan gravitates towards, and try to place the selected friend or acquaintance next to the guest of honour.

YOUR GUESTS

Virgoans like good listeners—and Taureans can be very good listeners, and they share the Virgo appreciation of harmony. Ask some imaginative Pisceans too, and some unconventional Aquarians, for they make good foils for the more inhibited Virgoan. But be sure to include some other Virgoans. They understand and like one another—their patience and industry, their critical ability, and their pleasure in country pursuits. To widen your guest list, ask a few Geminians—mercurial people, certainly, but good company when in form—and some Capricorns, who make trusty friends.

LUCKY DAYS

The lucky days for a Virgoan party are the fifth of the month or a Tuesday.

VIRGOAN CHARACTERISTICS

The Virgo people you will enjoy entertaining are the ones you find discriminating, appreciative of the fine arts, elegant, self-reliant, perceptive, gentle and kind. They will have a deep sense of responsibility—and a sense of fun, and a charm that will last till the end of their days. They are very generous to anyone in trouble—and they have a smile and a laugh that will lighten the blackest cloud!

The Virgoans you will not invite are the ones you find intolerant, opinionated, restless, vacillating, too undemonstrative, too conservative, too easily influenced, slaves to their medicine chests—and very apt to 'put on an act' if they want to get out of doing something. (It is just their gift for acting taking a wrong turn.)

As to their love life, Virgoans are both flirtatious and choosey. They like someone to make decisions for them, someone steadfast and intelligent. So though they may flirt at your party, they will not commit themselves on impulse, but go away and daydream about their romantic prospects in private enjoyment.

ICE-BREAKER

Most Virgoans have a sense of humour, and they are capable people who cook well. (Their kitchens will often smell delicious—it is one of their gifts.)

So, for your party, make them the famous 'scripture cake', and see if they can puzzle out the ingredients. If they can, they will have proved they know their Bible— and the cake will provide them with a welcome 'conversation piece' to help them over the first shy moments of the party.

Here is the recipe:

Ingredients

4½ cups of	I Kings iv 22	(1½lb flour)
1½ cups of	Judges v 25	(12oz butter)
2 cups of	Jeremiah vi 20	(14oz sugar)
2 cups of	I Samuel xxv 18	(12oz raisins)
2 cups of	Nahum iii 12	(12oz figs, chopped)
1 cup of	Numbers xvii 8	(4½oz shredded almonds)
2 tablespoons of	I Samuel xiv 25	(honey, warmed slightly)
6	Jeremiah xvii 11	(eggs)
1 pinch of	Leviticus ii 13	(salt)
1 cup of	Judges iv 19 (last clause)	(milk—8 fl oz)
3 teaspoons of	Amos iv 5	(baking powder)

Method

Follow Solomon's prescription for the making of a good boy and you will have a good cake. See Proverbs xxiii 14 —'Beat well'. To bring the method up to date: sieve the flour, salt and baking powder. Beat the butter and sugar to a cream, add the eggs one by one, beating each in well, and adding a spoonful of flour if the mixture seems inclined to curdle. Stir in the flour alternately with the milk, and add the honey. The mixture should be moist enough to drop heavily from a spoon. Add the rest of the ingredients and mix well. Put into a greased, paper-lined tin and bake in a moderate oven for about one hour—or until firm to the touch.

A professional cook tried out this cake for me. It works perfectly!

LUCKY STONES

For a special gift for a special Virgoan, choose one of their special stones—an emerald, diamond, pearl or jade.

The papal ring bears an emerald—a useful stone, as it is said to turn pale in the presence of treachery and deception. Diamonds bestow constancy and courage, while at one time a dissolved pearl was an ingredient of every love charm, and powdered pearls were prescribed as an antidote to poison.

Jade was endowed with even greater properties, for it was believed to have the power to raise the dead. A jade cup was said to crack if it came in contact with poison. Jade will also ward off lightning, and, if thrown into the sea, will instantly summon up mist, rain or snow. To the Chinese, jade united in itself the five cardinal virtues of charity, modesty, courage, justice and wisdom. It has always been regarded as a luck-bringer.

Virgoans' ruling planet is Mercury, whose colours are silvery white and pale blue, and other soft pale colours, including lavender.

PRESENTS FOR VIRGOANS

Virgoans love travel—but hate travelling in a muddle as much as they hate living in a muddle. So good presents would be 'travel accessories', such as a jewellery case, a hold-all to carry their sewing and their book, a rug, or lots of crisp tissue paper to help with their packing. Both men and women are perfectionists. Women love doing gros point and petit point, so give them a stamped canvas to embroider, or skeins of tapestry wool, or a silver thimble to ease their stitches.

To help keep a Virgoan home tidy, a magazine rack or a record rack would make an ideal present. All Virgoans are avid readers. They can whisk through a book a day and still extract all the essentials. So give them books— on travel, or to travel with—or a subscription to a magazine. They will often prefer overseas magazines, for they so enjoy travel, and after their travels are over, they will enjoy looking at magazines that help them relive their pleasure in foreign countries.

Though all Virgoans love a touch of luxury (*more* than a touch if possible) they are essentially realists, so they will be happier with tweeds and cashmeres than with more frivolous clothes. Many Virgoans have lovely homes, with furniture, tableware, lamps and ornaments all chosen with great taste. A Virgo man would appreciate a handsome decanter, or a really good tool for his workshop (where he will probably have a shadow board to keep everything tidy).

Virgoans have great sympathy for everything small and helpless, so you could safely trust them with a kitten or a puppy. In fact, such a present helps to bring out the warmth latent in so many Virgoans.

(Your young Virgoan friends will also love a small animal or bird, and the care of such creatures will help in their happy development. They love books, and will enjoy keeping them tidy in their own bookshelves. Cameras would make good presents for Virgoan children too; so would word games.)

The lucky metals for Virgoans are platinum and silver,

and you can be as luxurious and indulgent as you like
with presents embodying these two luck-bringers.

LUCKY PERFUMES

Choose 'light' scents for Virgoans, such as eau de
Cologne and toilet waters.

LUCKY FLOWERS AND TREES

Lavender is a plant that brings luck to Virgoans; a
little lavender bag to tuck under their pillow will bring
them pleasant dreams, and a sprig worn under the hat
will dispel headaches. The Phoenicians, Egyptians, Greeks
and Romans all loved lavender, and they burnt lavender
as incense. It is a lucky plant to have in your garden.

Another lucky flower for Virgoans is lily of the valley.
The juice from the stem was once prescribed to cure a
serpent's bite. Charlemagne regarded these lilies and
roses as the two most important plants in his model
garden in which he cultivated spices and medicinal herbs.

Maidenhair fern is also lucky for Virgoans. It can act
as a charm against witchcraft or be woven into a wreath
to cure headaches. Some say that the seed, if gathered on
Midsummer's Eve, will make you invisible, and burning
ferns will drive out serpents.

Another luckbringer for Virgo people is a carnation. In
Italy carnations were once made into coronets and garlands known as *corona,* and the flowers, first known in
England as 'coronations', gradually came to be called
'carnations'. They are said to have sprung from the tears
shed by the Virgin Mary on her way to Calvary. In spite
of this sad origin, carnations are lucky flowers.

HERBS AND FOODS

Herbs to ensure the well-being of Virgoans are marjoram, dill and chicory.

Greeks called marjoram 'the joy of the mountains', and it is a joy to cook with pork, poultry and game. It was also revered as a herb of happiness and was woven into sweet-smelling wreaths to crown young lovers. A spray kept in the dairy will prevent milk going sour in a thunderstorm.

Dill came to England with the Romans, and in the Middle Ages many people kept sprays of the lacy leaves as a protection against witches. Magicians and physicians also used dill for its stimulant and stomachic properties, and the oil was (and still is) used as a scent. Early American settlers called dill seeds 'meeting-house seeds', as they chumped and chewed them to help them through the boredom of long sermons.

Chicory is one of the magic medicinal herbs. In certain circumstances, a chicory leaf can open locked boxes. Served in a cup of tea, it is good for dyspeptics. A decoction of 1oz of chicory root added to 1 pint of boiling water was an old cure for jaundice, gout and rheumatism—and if you distrusted your doctor and all his bitter chicory medicine, you could escape the unpleasant consequences of his prescribing by using chicory to make you invisible!

Best foods for Virgoans are tomatoes, carrots, citrus fruit, apples, cauliflowers, asparagus, mushrooms, strawberries, figs, parsnips, dates, celery, endive and hazel nuts.

If you are serving coffee at the end of the party, serve with it one of the citrus fruit liqueurs—curaçao, grand marnier or vanderhum.

Libra

The Scales   23rd September to 22nd October

Giving a party for a Libran?

People born under this sign are often 'champagne' people—sparkling, elegant, lively—and the party they will enjoy best will be a lavish party at an expensive restaurant with everyone elegantly dressed. But really they will enjoy *any* party that gives them the chance to meet new and interesting fellow guests—and plenty of time to eat, drink—and especially to be merry.

YOUR GUESTS

Librans often have a real gift for friendship. They are essentially gregarious people, but clever and discriminating, and at times can be as choosey as a Virgoan. So select your guests with care, including some Aquarians (whose intuitive understanding intrigues Librans), and some Geminians, who, like Librans, revel in meeting new people. Include some amusing Ariens, some generous and inventive Leos, and some of the versatile Sagittarians. They combine to make the ingredients for a super party.

LUCKY DAYS

For a Libran celebration, choose the sixth of the month, or a Friday, which is their lucky day of the week.

LIBRAN CHARACTERISTICS

There will be Librans you like and Librans you do not like. They are people who have their ups and downs, for the scales are not necessarily evenly balanced all the time. They can be as sweet as honey or contrary as a mule, but in their happy moods they are delightful companions.

So invite Librans whom you find affectionate, appreciative of words, music, a quick quip or an art collection, original, fair-minded—possessing a gift for creating harmony, and as honest as the day.

Avoid the Librans who annoy you by being patronising, lazy, too gregarious, unwilling to make decisions, fair-minded to the point of aggravation, and either too anxious to please or full of sweet unreasonableness.

As for their love life, Librans wholeheartedly enjoy being in love, and throughout their lives it is a subject—or a state of mind—that never loses its appeal. Love-making is an art many Librans excel at, and as they are generally attractive to the opposite sex, they may very likely leave the party with a new admirer.

ICE-BREAKER

Librans are not shy people. They are poised and self-confident, but a party ice-breaker may help the less assured guests.

Librans are often very sophisticated, but nevertheless they have a particular affinity with nature, and for their party nothing would please them more than to be taught something of the language of flowers.

At one time this was a language that everyone understood, and there are many references in Shakespeare to the symbolism of flowers, which he obviously expected his audiences to understand.

For instance, a columbine was regarded as the symbol of a discarded lover. In *Hamlet* act IV scene 5 Ophelia joins it with fennel and rue, two plants emblematic of sorrow:

'There's fennel for you, and columbines: there's
rue for you: and here's some for me.'

Ophelia also says: 'And there is pansies—that's for
thoughts'— a meaning still associated with pansies, a word
derived from the French word, *pensée*, a thought.

Tell Librans how to make a lover's bouquet of irises ('I
send you a message'), honeysuckle ('of generous and
devoted affection'), include violets for 'faithfulness',
poppies, which say 'my dreams are of you', and jasmine,
which signifies 'our love will be sweet'.

As a full stop to your lover's message, add a camellia.
That will say, 'I shall love you always'.

Let us hope that the loved one thus addressed in the
language of flowers knows a suitable floral answer: a
bunch of daisies—'I share your sentiments'. (Of course,
the answer might be an uncompromising anemone—'Go
away!')

LUCKY STONES

Stones specially lucky for your special Libran guest are
lapis lazuli, opals and coral.

Lapis lazuli is an interesting stone—rich blue in colour
with golden flecks of pyrites. In the Middle Ages, it was
powdered and added to paints—and to lapis lazuli is due
the glorious unfading blues used by the Old Masters. This
stone was once placed in embalmed bodies, to represent
the hearts, which were always removed. It was said to
counteract the wiles of the Devil and ensure help from the
angels.

Opals dispel melancholy and sadness. They were once
greatly treasured by thieves, as they were believed to
make their wearer invisible. Opals could calm tempests,
staunch blood and give wisdom.

Librans' ruling planets are Venus and Saturn. Venus's

colour is blue—a colour signifying love and affection. Saturn's colours are all very dark. Blues are luckiest for Librans.

PRESENTS FOR LIBRANS

All Librans delight in presents, but they would rather have no present than one that does not measure up to their high standards of taste.

They love the feel, the look and the smell of leather-bound books or pigskin gloves, and gifts that add to the elegance of their homes, such as a desk set or a handsome blotter, or opera glasses (for they are keen theatre and opera goers). Books on home decorating or travel would be appropriate gifts for these people. So would books of poetry, or Roget's *Thesaurus of English Words and Phrases*. Other suitable presents would be nicely framed prints, or a record-player to supply the soft music most Librans like as a background to their lives.

Women take pride in their appearance, and, like Taurean girls, if you give a Libran girl a gift of money, you can trust her to come home with exquisite undies, gossamer-soft bedjackets, lovely linen, lovely candlesticks, or pretty accessories for her bedroom. Of course, you could buy her any one of these luxuries for her as a present, or just yards of pretty ribbon to thread through her lingerie.

All Librans enjoy special occasions—so what about a gift of theatre tickets? Good ones, please!

(Young Libran girls like ribbons, flowers for their hats or their hair, and bubble baths. Boys will like a T-shirt or a camera. Both like books—and rather too many choco-lates for their own good!)

The lucky metal for Librans is copper—a wonderful excuse for browsing in an antique shop, or among street market-stalls, for a copper kettle, a coal scuttle, or even a hunting horn!

LUCKY PERFUMES

Lotus lily is one of the Libran scents. Others are wild orchid, gardenia and jasmine.

LUCKY FLOWERS AND TREES

Trees are luckier for Librans than flowers, and their special trees are ash, elm and birch. Gladioli are also fortunate for Librans; so are asters. They are flowers that are associated with Venus, and thus with Librans. Like daisies, asters can be used for the old, old game 'he loves me, he loves me not'. When you know the answer, gather up all the petals and burn them. The fire will drive away serpents.

Gipsies believe that the Cross was made of an ash-tree, and because of this the tree has acquired many virtues. Ash-trees were planted in sacred groves in Scandinavia, where it was known as the 'world tree' and called by its holy name, Iggdrasil. The 'world tree' had its roots in the underworld and its branches in the heavens. It thus bound together heaven, hell and earth. Witches hated the ash-tree, though they made the handles of their brooms from it as this magical tree preserved even witches from drowning.

Elm smoke has a valuable property. Cattle driven through the smoke will be cured of any disease.

Give your Libran guests a sprig of birch to wear on the night of the party. It will protect them from the Evil Eye and will act as a safeguard against wounds, gout, jaundice, barrenness—and caterpillars. The protective powers of birch-trees are so effective that country people made besom brooms of birch twigs to sweep witches away from their neighbourhood.

HERBS AND FOODS

The best herbs for Librans are watercress, lemon balm, and thyme.

Watercress improves the complexion; it cures impurities of the blood, and, because of its vitamin and iron content, is an excellent salad ingredient. Watercress was known in ancient Egypt, in Persia and in Greece. The Greeks had a proverb: 'Eat cress and get wit.'

Lemon balm was one of the favourites of the old herb gardens, and lemon balm tea, made by infusing four fresh leaves in a pint of boiling water, was believed to strengthen the memory and chase away melancholy. It is still used (with lemon juice) as a refreshing summer drink.

Thyme was regarded by the ancient Greeks as a symbol of courage and vitality. They burnt it as an incense in their temples, and made thyme vinegar to relieve their headaches. The Romans brought thyme to England—and in the days of high chivalry, it was once again regarded as a symbol of courage. A sprig was often given to knights by their ladies, or embroidered on scarves given to lords and lovers setting out for the wars. Rudyard Kipling, in his poem 'Sussex', described thyme as smelling 'like dawn in Paradise'.

There is a great variety of foods especially good for Librans, including apples, quinces, strawberries, raspberries, figs, pomegranates, peaches, celery, beetroot, spinach, peas, sweet corn, raisins and almonds.

Apples, for hundreds of years, have been regarded as the sacred fruit of Britain. Though few fruits were cultivated until the sixteenth century, costard apples were being sold in England in the thirteenth century. Shakespeare mentions many different varieties of apples, including codlings, pippins, leather coats (now known as russets), apple-johns, bitter sweets, pomewaters and costards. The costard was a popular cooking apple in his day. Today their name remains in the word 'costermonger' (now a synonym for a Pearlie King).

Librans should eat five almonds a day to prevent intoxication.

With the coffee, serve one of the citrus fruit liqueurs—curaçao, grand marnier, or vanderhum—or be more original, and serve calvados, an apple-based liqueur (so much enjoyed by Superintendent Maigret).

Scorpio

The Scorpion   23rd October to 21st November

Giving a party for a Scorpio?

Scorpios can be both gourmets and gourmands, so prepare good food and plenty of it. Like Leos, they appreciate good wine to drink, and good, substantial food cooked in wine.

Scorpios make good public speakers, and they like to talk wherever they are. They like lots of attention, but they are good companions, and attract people through their mental agility.

So do not aim at too formal a party, but ask intelligent guests—and give them all plenty of time to talk their heads off!

YOUR GUESTS

To meet your Scorpio friend, invite some other Scorpios, because they appreciate one another's intelligence and understand that each of them is likely to have a secret side to their life kept entirely hidden from the world. Also ask some of the tranquil Cancerians (good foils for the dramatic Scorpios), some adaptable Pisceans (who can shine at any party), and some considerate Taureans and Leos, the other gourmets of the Zodiac (and Leos can be as shrewd as Scorpios, and can encourage their ambition, which sometimes needs a spur). And, for good measure, invite some philosophical Capricorns, and affectionate Virgoans.

LUCKY DAYS

Lucky days for a Scorpio party are the ninth of the month—or a Tuesday.

SCORPIO CHARACTERISTICS

Many Scorpios have strong, magnetic personalities, and though they like to talk, they can make their presence felt without saying anything at all! They have great potential for sexual attraction, whether they put on all the glamour or wear old jeans. They are often highly intelligent, with great emotional depth.

For your party, ask the Scorpios you find honest and warm, generous in repaying a kindness, shrewd and observant, considerate, with a humanitarian outlook on life, loyal, versatile—and excellent peacemakers.

The ones you will not invite to your party are the Scorpios who (to you) are neurotic, bitter, arrogant, over-critical, selfish, jealous—with a streak of cunning or cruelty if you get on the wrong side of them. They are people who *must* win.

As to their love-life, Scorpios have no time for flirtations, and shy away from anyone who shows signs of possessiveness. Once they have made up their minds about a marriage partner, only Heaven can make them change. So forget any ideas you might have about match-making and get on with the party.

ICE-BREAKER

Many Scorpios have mystical gifts, and most of them at some time in their lives will be interested in astrology or numerology. So there could be nothing better as an ice-breaker for Scorpio guests than to show everyone at the party how to work out their lucky numbers.

Numerology is one of the oldest branches of occult

practice. The 'science' of numerology is founded on the belief that in common with jewels, wood, and other inanimate objects, numbers can give out favourable or unfavourable vibrations that can influence the lives of the people concerned.

The numbers 1 to 9 are mainly used by numerologists, though there are other, more complicated systems.

A simple way of finding your guest's harmonious number is to add the numbers of his complete birthday—day, month and year, going on adding till you reach the single lucky number.

However, many of your guests may be shy about telling you their birth date. Then you can work out their lucky number by the numerical value of the letters of their name, choosing the name by which they are usually known. As an example, say your guest of honour's name is Patricia Ann Jones, usually known as Patsy.

From time immemorial, different numbers have been given to the letters of the alphabet (or perhaps, letters have been given to numbers, once regarded as all-powerful, and therefore more safely referred to by 'code' letters, just as it was considered unlucky to speak directly of the Devil, who was therefore referred to obliquely as 'Old Nick' or 'Old Scratch').

One of the most generally accepted tables of letter values is this:

A	- 1	H	- 8	O	- 7	TH	- 8
B	- 2	I	- 1	P	- 8	U	- 6
C	- 2	J	- 1	PH	- 9	V	- 6
D	- 4	K	- 2	Q	- 1	W	- 6
E	- 5	L	- 3	R	- 2	X	- 6
F	- 8	M	- 4	S	- 3	Y	- 1
G	- 3	N	- 5	T	- 4	Z	- 7

Your friend's 'active' name (as it is called)—Patsy—is the important one. The numbers representing this are: P-8; A-1; T-4; S-3; Y-1; total: 17. So her lucky number is 8.

LUCKY STONES

As well as a number of lucky stones, Scorpios have a special amulet all their own—a bracelet or ring in the shape of a serpent. Many Scorpios have the gift of healing—and healing has been connected with the wisdom of the serpent for thousands of years.

Scorpios' ruling planet is Mars—the same as for Ariens. So all red stones are lucky for Scorpios, including garnets, bloodstones, and rubies as well as aquamarines and beryls.

A ruby will warn the wearer of approaching evil by turning dark—but this should never happen, for tradition says that the owner of a ruby will live at peace with the world, secure in his rank and free from all sadness.

Aquamarines are bringers of help and good health, and are especially lucky for ocean-going travellers. Beryls will help Scorpios in battles or litigation, make them invisible, and cure their laziness.

PRESENTS FOR SCORPIOS

If you do not want to give your Scorpio guest of honour one of their lucky jewels, a modern steel ring set with a highly-polished red stone would be most acceptable.

All Scorpios—men, women, boys and girls—live partly in a secret world, so give them a diary with a lock—or a box with a lock in which they can keep some of their secrets secret.

They are people who thrive on excitement and drama,

and situations that would dismay others are the very ones they thrive on. They love exciting colours, bold patterns, good living. So give them a striking scarf or shirt, or a bottle of superb wine, or some gourmet food. Both men and women will enjoy a gourmet cook book, exotic spice and copper kitchenware. Women will appreciate an eye-catching apron (they like to be eye-catching), some un-usual scent, or a dramatic piece of junk jewellery. Men are clever with machinery, so give them tools for their workshop or some new mechanical gadget.

Other good presents for Scorpios are books on witches, ghosts, and ancient civilisations (which fascinate them). As they are usually devoted to their families, a 'family tree' of tiny picture frames to hold photographs or minia-tures would be an ideal present.

(Your young Scorpio friends will like magic kits, chemistry sets, and something to occupy their talented hands. Girls would love a sewing machine. They will probably also enjoy historical romances.)

The lucky metal for Scorpios is steel, so you could give them steel salt and pepper shakers, teapot and jug, elegant steel cuff-links, or a set of kitchen knives for their gourmet cooking.

LUCKY PERFUMES

Perfumes most Scorpios like are sophisticated and sultry—musk, magnolia and attar of roses. Some will also like lily of the valley.

LUCKY FLOWERS AND TREES

Anemones, with their bright gipsy colouring, are one of the lucky flowers for Scorpios; so are gentians, gorse, celandines, and scarlet pimpernels.

Anemones are said to have been brought to Europe by

the Crusaders embedded in soil from the Holy Land. In ancient Rome, chewing anemone roots was advised for anyone with toothache, and a 'brew' of roots and boiling water was used to treat the scars of wounds.

All the gentians are beautiful. Some of those grown in Austria are gathered to make a liqueur. The English varieties can be made into a tisane—good for tummyache and fainting. As for gorse, legend says that love will flourish as long as gorse blooms, and as it is always blooming somewhere, the world seems pretty safe for lovers.

Celandines are an interesting example of the medieval 'doctrine of signatures'. This theory held that all plants carried on them some indication of their medicinal value —for those clever enough to read the signs. Hence celandines, yellow in themselves, and whose stems when broken, exude an orange juice, were considered a cure for jaundice.

The scarlet pimpernel is another example of nature 'pointing the way' to those with wisdom. As the petals are red, and blood is red, the scarlet pimpernel was used to staunch blood from an open wound. It was also prescribed as an antidote to the bites of insects and venomous snakes.

There is a rhyme about these flowers:

> No ear hath heard
> No tongue can tell
> The virtues of the pimpernel.

HERBS AND FOODS

Among the herbs and spices especially beneficial to Scorpios are basil, rosemary, allspice and ginger.

'Sweet basil' is a native of India, where it is considered a holy herb. In Europe, it was regarded as a protection against witchcraft, and when powdered, used as snuff.

Rosemary was a holy and magical plant. It could evoke love and renew youth. It was strewn in rooms to keep the air sweet and to protect them against bad fairies, and it was burnt in sickrooms to dispel infection. Rosemary also signified wisdom, love and loyalty, and a few chopped leaves were always added to wedding cakes. Rosemary wood was chosen to make lutes.

Allspice, which combines the flavour of cloves, cinnamon and nutmeg, was once necessary for the preservation of meat, particularly wild pigs. The meat so cured was called 'boucan'. Because of pirates' reliance on boucan during their long expeditions at sea, they became known as boucaneers, or buccaneers. Oil obtained from the leaves of allspice is used in medicine as a stimulant.

Ginger, in the Middle Ages, was highly prized and very expensive. It was a rich man's spice, and 1lb of ginger was worth a whole sheep. The first 'gingerbread' was probably baked two thousand years before Christ—unleavened, and sweetened with honey—in Rhodes. Ships called at the island specially to buy this pungent bread, and it was one of the favourite recipes cooked in monasteries, for monastery gardens were among the first places where costly spices of all kinds were available. Elizabeth I employed a special artist-cum-baker to create gingerbread lords and ladies.

Scorpios have good appetites. Give them plenty of leeks and onions, asparagus, rhubarb, cabbage, cheese and cream cheese, black cherries, gooseberries, coconut, oranges, lemons, mandarins, grapefruit and raisins.

When you are serving coffee, offer preserved ginger—an epicurean delight—or ginger chocolates. And for a liqueur, you have a choice of maraschino or kirsch, both of which are based on cherries—one of the Scorpio fruits.

Sagittarius

The Archer   22nd November to 22nd December

Giving a party for a Sagittarian?

Sagittarians like a reason for a party, but it is no hardship thinking up a reason to entertain these candid, generous people. Besides they are such excellent hosts when it is their turn to give a party. Most Sagittarians are very conscious of their near-association with Christmas, so there is a ready-made excuse. Invite them to your first Christmas party, and serve the first mince pies of the season. (They like background music. At *this* party it could be softly played carols.)

YOUR GUESTS

To meet your Sagittarian guest of honour, invite some Geminians, whose many interests will be sure to give them something in common. In fact, like Gemini people, Sagittarians often have two strong interests going at the same time, and they will make a success of whatever they do wholeheartedly. Also ask some lively Ariens (for Sagittarians are quick-witted people who appreciate a nimble wit in others)—some of the good-hearted Leos, and some Librans. They are good guests at any party—happy party-goers who enjoy practically any entertainment. And ask some other Sagittarians—ones who share an interest with your principal guest, such as music, or the theatre, or sport (usual Sagittarian hobbies). All your guests for your Sagittarian party should be intelligent and well-informed.

LUCKY DAYS

Hold your party on the third of the month, or on a Thursday, the lucky day for Sagittarians.

SAGITTARIAN CHARACTERISTICS

With the best will in the world, no one can like everyone. The Sagittarians you will want to ask to your party are the ones you find enterprising, humorous, generous, warm-hearted, versatile, fearless, idealistic, cheerfully optimistic, and at times endearingly quixotic.

The Sagittarians you do not like (and would not ask to any party) are those you find too outspoken, too high-minded for anybody's comfort, too critical, restless, snobbish, tight-fisted, quick to take offence—and sometimes quite outrageous.

Sagittarians have a reputation for 'marrying in haste and repenting in leisure'. So do not become involved in your guest of honour's love life. Let well alone. Do not try any match-making. It may be held against you later on. The best marriage a Sagittarian can make is one he has decided on for himself. (Most Sagittarians are flirts, anyway.)

ICE-BREAKER

There is no reason to think of an ice-breaker for a Sagittarian party—as some of your Sagittarian guests will be delighted to break the ice themselves—by reading tea-cups!

But they like a bit of fun, so let all your guests play the old December game of Snapdragon and join in the chorus of the old doggerel verse—and give a fun present to whoever pulls out most raisins.

Place a lot of raisins in a large bowl, which should be wide and shallow. Slightly warm some brandy, pour it over the raisins, and set it alight. Hold the bowl for your guests, who must snatch as many raisins as they can. Turn out the lights for the full effect of this game—a relic of Druid fire-worship—and as your guests scorch their fingers, recite the old verses known as 'The Song of the Snapdragon'.

Here he comes with flaming bowl,
Don't he mean to take his toll, snip, snap, dragon!
With his blue and lapping tongue
Many of you will be stung, snip, snap, dragon!
For he snaps at all that comes
Snatching at his feast of plums, snip, snap, dragon!

LUCKY STONES

For a special occasion (and it is sure to be a special occasion, so near Christmas), give your Sagittarian guest a gift embodying one of their lucky stones—an amethyst, a topaz, a sapphire (a protection against ill omens and the Evil Eye), or a chrysolite (which will break enchantments and put evil spirits to flight).

An amethyst is a symbol of sincerity. It gives the wearer peace of mind and is a protection against neuralgia —and intoxication. Amethysts are often set in episcopal rings, so the stones are associated with blessings, and will ensure true and everlasting love.

A topaz brings love and affection, cures anger, and is a protection against the effects of poison.

Sagittarians' ruling planet is Jupiter, influenced to some extent by Mars. Jupiter bestows generosity and good humour. Mars gives Sagittarians energy, and spurs them to battle for other people's rights.

PRESENTS FOR SAGITTARIANS

Sagittarians have a particular love of animals, so give them a book about their favourite pets—or a present for the pet! Most of them enjoy sports, and they will appreciate a gift on their current interest. But check before you buy, for they change from one hobby to another at a moment's notice, and it may be horse-riding this week and golf next. They also enjoy camping, and camping equipment would always be received with warm thanks.

Although they dislike housework, they love entertaining, and make excellent hosts and hostesses, and welcome presents that help to make for a smooth-running and enjoyable party, such as bar accessories, lovely glasses or unusual party food, or a beautifully turned wooden salad bowl.

Sagittarian women like classic clothes, and both men and women like chunky sweaters, real leather belts, or wallets. They like functional gifts—and they like tickets to an opera, ballet or symphony concert. As many of them are gamblers (and lucky) you could give them a pack of cards to play poker with, or buy some gambling game they could play at home.

(Young Sagittarians are good mixers, and enjoy school, and presents to do with school or sport. Or give them an encyclopaedia so that they can find out for themselves the answers to some of the everlasting questions they ask. They like animals too, and books about animals.)

Sagittarians' lucky metal is tin, which gives you plenty of scope for presents—tins of luxury food, a set of canisters, a tin of biscuits or a modern alarm clock.

LUCKY PERFUMES

Luck-bringing scents for Sagittarians are white stock, verbena and heather.

LUCKY FLOWERS AND TREES

Lucky flowers for Sagittarians are all the purple and mauve flowers—irises, violets, African violets, mauve delphiniums, lavender, violas—and the deep, bright gold of dandelions.

But one plant particularly appropriate for a Christmas-time party is particularly lucky for Sagittarians, and this is mistletoe, the 'golden bough' of classical legend, and the wonder-working plant of the Druids. Mistletoe (like holly and ivy) was regarded as a life symbol because it flowers in the winter. Mistletoe was once called 'all-heal', for it not only cured all kinds of ailments, but resolved quarrels between enemies. In Scandinavia, a branch of mistletoe hung outside a house promised a safe welcome, and if enemies met under a tree bearing mistletoe, they had to lay down their arms and fight no more that day. Though still regarded as a pagan plant, and never used in church decorations, mistletoe is one of the favourite house decorations at Christmas time, and especially appropriate for Sagittarians as a bringer of luck and fertility, while mistletoe tea will counteract the venomous bites of all sorts of creatures—and cure toothache.

Oak-trees also bring luck to Sagittarians, and an acorn worn as a charm will preserve their youthfulness. Oaks were deeply revered by the Druids, partly because they served as host trees to the sacred mistletoe, and also because they were thought to provide protection against thunder and thunderbolts. (Druids ate the acorns of their sacred oaks to induce the right mood for prophesying.) Gipsies believe that a necklace of acorns—dried and pierced with red-hot knitting needles, threaded together and worn day and night—will cure indigestion and all weaknesses of the stomach.

HERBS AND FOODS

Herbs that are beneficial to Sagittarians are sage, marjoram and mallows. Dandelions are good for these people too. The leaves are rich in vitamins A and D and are excellent in salads or cooked like spinach.

Sage grows best for the wise, as rosemary grows best for the righteous. It was once thought that sage tea made men prudent and long-lived, that it cured dyspepsia, strengthened the memory, and cured sore throats, rheumatism, ulcers, consumption and snake-bites. The English drank sage tea long before China tea, and the Chinese liked it so well that they traded 3lb of their tea for every 1lb of sage. It is still enjoyed as a stimulating drink. It can be sweetened with honey and spiced with rum.

Marjoram was one of the 'strewing herbs' in Tudor and Stuart times and housewives used the flowers to dye wool purple and linen a reddish-brown. The Greeks prescribed it as an antidote for poisoning and dropsy—and crowned young lovers with marjoram wreaths.

Mallow flowers (made into a tisane) were an old cottage remedy for colds and sore throats. The roots were boiled with a handful of raisins—and a drink of this decoction would give protection against all diseases all day long. Mallows were once mixed with thrushes, dates, snails, pine kernels, and many other strange ingredients to make a stuffing for roast pigs eaten at Roman feasts.

As for foods, Sagittarians never seem to grow tired of strawberries. They also enjoy asparagus, bilberries, chestnuts, onions, parsnips, prunes, apples, cherries, wild rice, red cabbage, chicory, corn on the cob, barley, endive, limes, figs and cucumbers.

With your coffee, serve one of the appropriate liqueurs —calvados (which has an apple base), or one of the cherry-based favourites, maraschino and kirsch.

Capricorn

The Goat   23rd December to 19th January

Giving a party for a Capricorn?

Capricorns are out-of-doors people, and fresh air is very necessary for them, so suggest a picnic party (with substantial foods, as they have lively appetites). As they also love horse-racing, you could combine two of their loves and take a picnic to a race meeting. It need not be the Derby or Royal Ascot. They will enjoy a local point-to-point just as much, or a polo match, as their love of horses is part of their enjoyment.

YOUR GUESTS

Cancerians, who share the Capricorn pleasure in travel, will make good fellow guests. Also invite some easy-going, artistic Librans and some jovial Sagittarians. Other guests should include some animal-loving Taureans, and some Virgoans, whose down-to-earth outlook matches the Capricorns' qualities of practical honesty. Ask a few intellectual Geminians—but avoid the superficial ones, as Capricorns respect intellect but turn away from any form of artificiality. Include some fellow Capricorns. They understand one another's direct outlook on life.

LUCKY DAYS

The lucky days for Capricorns are the eighth of the month, or Saturdays.

CAPRICORN CHARACTERISTICS

The Capricorns you will want to ask to your party are

the ones you find warm-hearted, diplomatic, good organisers, protective, independent, and with a great feeling for the arts. They expand wonderfully when shown affection, they make faithful friends and are charming and popular guests, and they are often wise people.

The Capricorn people you will not want to invite are those you consider to be brusque, too outspoken, moody, easily discouraged, unscrupulous in attaining their ambitions, interfering in other people's business, patronising and snobbish.

Capricorns are inclined to take life seriously, but they nevertheless enjoy flirtations, and trying to organise other people's love lives. They are not usually demonstrative, so do not embarrass them by introducing them to an 'obvious' marriage partner. They like to marry well—so leave them to make their own choice.

ICE-BREAKER

There is not much need of an ice-breaker at a picnic. If you go to a race meeting, you can add a little excitement by running a sweepstake on the main event. The 'subscription' can be as little as you like, but even if the winner wins no more than a few pence, it gives a sense of occasion and adds a sting of excitement to the outing.

But if it is raining, and you decide to follow the races on your television set, the 'Luck of the Draw' is a good way to loosen tongues and to test your guests' luck for the next few days.

Hand your guest a pack of cards to shuffle, and then lay them out to form a 'pyramid', with one card at the top, then two, then three, and so on till the last line contains seven cards. (There will be twenty-eight cards altogether.) Now look at the suits. If Hearts predominate, your guest's luck will be excellent. If Clubs predominate, the luck will be good, if Diamonds, fair, and Spades mean your guest will have to be patient. Luck is a bit elusive at the moment. (If two suits should tie, turn up the remaining cards one at a time till one suit wins.)

LUCKY STONES

Capricorns are very conscious of 'luck', and as they are so fond of horses, give them a tiny horseshoe to hang from a key ring, or one of their fortunate stones—moonstones, jacinths (worn by travellers to assure them a welcome at any inn, to protect them against capture, the plague, and lightning), and pearls.

Moonstones are full of magic, and if you hold one in your mouth at the time of the full moon, it will enable you to see into the future. It is a stone that evokes tender passions, brings good luck to its owner, cures epilepsy and nervousness—and if hung on a fruit-tree, will ensure a good crop!

White stones, such as moonstones and pearls, denote purity, and an amulet set with pearls will give Capricorns purity of thought.

Capricorns' ruling planet is Saturn, and though Saturn's colours are dark brown and black, Capricorns should avoid these, as they may affect their natural tendency to depression. Tans and light browns, and blues of all shades are the lucky colours for Capricorns.

PRESENTS FOR CAPRICORNS

In spite of their cool exterior, Capricorns are devoted friends and family people, and they will love a photograph frame for some of their favourite photographs—a good plain leather one, nothing gimmicky for a Capricorn. They have a very good sense of values, and regard frivolous presents as a waste of money. So, for these people, choose fine quality towels, a 'sensible' pullover, sponge-able table mats, leather gloves, a classic never-dating handbag, a set of canisters or time and money saving gadgets.

Both men and women like comfort, so cushions would make good presents; so would table lamps, or a travelling rug. Many of them have a strong sense of history, and will enjoy books on historical themes, heraldry, or genealogy, or on the history of art or ballet. And they like antiques, good pictures, and ceramics.

(Young Capricorns soon develop an amazing memory, so give them books to stimulate their interests. Boys like carpentry, and a piggy bank to save up their money gifts. Girls like dolls' houses, which they will keep in apple-pie order—and paint-boxes.)

Capricorns' lucky metal is lead, but perhaps you could stretch a point and give your special Capricorn friend a gift of pewter.

LUCKY PERFUMES

Narcissus is a very special scent for Capricornians, who also like pine, frangipani, lilac, jasmine and rose.

LUCKY FLOWERS AND TREES

The lucky flowers for Capricorns include heartsease or wild pansy. (Shakespeare knew it as 'love-in-idleness' and in his time it was a popular ingredient of love potions.) Another lucky flower is the Christmas rose, once regarded as a cure for melancholy and a protection against evil spirits, though witches used it in many of their charms.

Chief bringer of luck to a Capricorn is an elder-tree—a favourite wood to make whistles from, useful to cure adder bites, toothache, saddle soreness and freckles, while the flowers make excellent fritters and a soothing tisane.

Elder-trees have always been treated with great respect in England because till quite recently it was believed that a dryad lived in their branches and avenged any injury done to the tree. So they were never cut for kindling. Sometimes witches hide in elder-trees, transforming themselves into branches. So never cut down an elder to make a baby's cradle, nor burn it in your hearth. But if you stand under an elder on Midsummer Night's Eve, you will see the King of the Elves ride past.

Walnut and quince trees are also lucky for Capricorns. All nuts were magical, and were often used in spells and divinations, and walnuts were particularly valued as an antidote to poison, and a necklace of walnuts would cure rheumatism.

Quinces were a love token in the ancient world, for traditionally a quince was the fruit given to Aphrodite by young Paris, son of Priam, king of Troy.

Honesty is said to grow only in the gardens of honest folk, and it grows well for Capricorns, and will keep them safe. The silver discs of honesty reflect any light shining on them—and shining lights put evil spirits to flight.

HERBS AND FOODS

Beneficial herbs for Capricorns are anise, bay and betony.

Anise was mentioned in an Egyptian herbal in 1500 B.C., and both Pliny and Charlemagne thought highly of this herb, which in the Middle Ages was one of the imports taxed by English kings. The seeds—aniseed—are still a popular additive to cakes, scent and cough mixtures. Some muscatels and vermouths are flavoured with dried anise flowers, and anise oil forms the base of the French liqueur anisette. Anise is a kindly herb. Hang a sprig over your bed. It will scare off nightmares.

To carry a sprig of bay guaranteed protection against poison and sorcery, and bay leaves were regarded as a great healer. Because of their association with good health and well-being, young doctors just through their exams were crowned with bay (or laurel) leaves—and hence became known as bacca-laureates, or bachelors. Heroes, poets and winners of games were also crowned with these laurel wreaths. Bay has always been a fortunate tree. Growing near a house, it affords protection against all kinds of trouble, including the plague, the Devil, thunder, lightning, snake-bites and caterpillars. Leaves placed under a pillow ensure pleasant dreams.

Erasmus, the great Dutch scholar and friend of Sir Thomas More, maintained that an amulet made of betony would 'drive away devils and despair'. Betony was widely cultivated in the gardens of apothecaries and monasteries. It was recommended for a score of complaints, including jaundice, gout, epidemic diseases, fistulas, belching, convulsions, nightmares and evil spirits, and, mixed with honey, it was an aid to childbirth. Its reputation was so high that the Italians had a saying about it: 'Sell your coat and buy betony.'

Capricorns share Sagittarians' love of strawberries. (As somebody said, 'Doubtless God Almighty could have made a better berry, but he never did'.) They should also eat quinces, beetroot, figs, plums, spinach, asparagus, cucumber, lettuce, coconut, almonds, rye bread and sea fish.

To serve with your coffee, offer your guests anisette—or slivovitz, the plum brandy.

Aquarius

The Water Bearer   20th January to 20th February

Giving a party for an Aquarian?

Aquarian people really prefer going to the theatre than to a party, but they would enjoy a supper party afterwards. They like meeting 'characters'—in fact they often attract them—and can be intrigued by unusual food.

They are often too reserved to be the easiest of guests, but they have the saving grace of being interested in people—individual people—and many of them have friends of all ages and from all strata. A buffet party is their ideal. If the guests are encouraged to serve themselves, it helps overcome the Aquarians' shyness. (Have a warm room; Aquarians feel the cold.)

YOUR GUESTS

To meet your Aquarian guests, ask some of their 'best friend' groups, enthusiastic Geminians and affectionate Librans. Also ask some Cancerians (to whom, like Aquarians, unexpected things happen, but hopefully not at your party), some dynamic Ariens, and some warm-hearted Sagittarians (who, like Aquarians, value personal liberty).

LUCKY DAYS

Best days for an Aquarian party are the fourth of the month, or a Friday.

AQUARIAN CHARACTERISTICS

Aquarians are mixtures. They can be funny, eccentric, practical, patient, impatient, exasperating, dashing and timid. You will like the Aquarians who are self-reliant, enthusiastic, courteous, imaginative, good friends and good companions, independent, with broad sympathies.

The Aquarians you would never invite to any party are those who procrastinate, are unreliable, discontented, slow to forgive, hypersensitive, too detached and eternally elusive.

As to their love life, Aquarians often carry their desire for freedom to such lengths as to take evasive action if matrimony is suggested. Even if you think you have finally leg-roped an Aquarian, you may still find he has quietly evaporated, unless matrimony is *his* decision.

ICE-BREAKER

Having once enticed your Aquarians to a party, you must think of some way of making them circulate, as they prefer to find some kindred spirit and stay put.

They are often intuitive readers of character, so introduce some palm reading. Once you start them off, they are quite capable of taking over, and soon will be circulating just to look at other guests' hands.

Buy a book on palmistry and swot up enough to sound authentic, and the party will soon be carried along on its own impetus!

First of all, ask your guest of honour to show you her hands, open and relaxed, palm upwards. Notice how the fingers lie in repose. A good space between the thumb and first finger means generosity and adaptability. Fingers held close together denote secrecy. When the little finger stands well apart, it indicates great independence. (Don't interfere!)

Long fingers that bend backwards show cleverness, a mind good at detail, but with no talent for money matters. A stiff thumb indicates stubbornness, a 'wasted' thumb denotes sympathy for all God's creatures, and 'knotted' finger joints are found on thoughtful and philosophical people.

Most people know the main lines of the hand—the heart, the head, the life and the fate lines. The best heart line begins between the first and second fingers. This shows a well-balanced person who will make a good companion and marriage partner. The head line and the life line usually start together. If they are separated, they indicate an excessive love of excitement. The life line encircles the thumb and the mount of Venus, and a good curve and a firm line mean good health with a love of activity. The fate line runs up from the wrist towards the middle finger. If it starts from the life line, it means that success will come through the family. If it starts independently, it indicates that determination is needed to bring success.

A square on the palm is a sign of preservation—from

illness or a catastrophe. 'Islands' on the heart line mean disappointments in love. Stars on the lines are a warning, but stars on the finger and thumb indicate good luck. By this time, everyone should be circulating, and you can safely retire to the kitchen to put the finishing touches to the food.

LUCKY STONES

Lucky stones for Aquarians are moonstones, onyx, rubies and topaz.

An onyx can bring courage and conjugal love, but do not wear it at night as a legend says that there is imprisoned in each onyx a demon that wakes at night and causes nightmares. However, moonstones—which hold the radiance of the moon—are said to banish nightmares and all evils of the night, so wearing a moonstone should cope with the demons!

Rubies bestow a gift of great importance to Aquarians —freedom. They also bestow charity and dignity, and guard the owner's house, his fruit-trees and his vineyards.

A topaz is symbolic of loyalty, assures long life, beauty and intelligence, and cures enchantment, insomnia—and wind. These beautiful stones range in colour from pale pink to a smoky brown. The national gem of Scotland, a cairngorm, is a topaz.

Aquarians' ruling planets are Saturn and Uranus. Saturn is often a hard task-master, and Aquarians often have to struggle to overcome many obstacles before achieving success. Their lucky colour is blue.

PRESENTS FOR AQUARIANS

Books of plays or theatre or ballet tickets would make excellent gifts for Aquarians. They also like presents that combine good design with usefulness. This could be anything from a well-made bird-table to a compact home filing system.

Sometimes they become so involved in their many interests that they forget they are still using accessories years old, so new scarves, gloves, ties, handbags or neck-laces will be appreciated both by the Aquarians and by their friends! They may like *avant garde* and very individual clothes—or the exact opposite.

All Aquarians like books, especially about their current interest, and books on small mammals and trees and their legends. Above all, they are interested in people, and as they are often fascinated by people who know secrets, they would enjoy books about doctors and medical dis-coveries, or on such themes as the secrets of Scotland Yard. It is the *personal* side of life that intrigues them.

Many Aquarians are also interested in photography and tape-recording.

(Your bright and mischievous young Aquarian friends will be interested in science, and would enjoy a chemistry set, a camera and developing equipment, or just a new film.)

The lucky metal for Aquarians is copper, which gives you plenty of scope for presents, from an 'anti-rheumatism' bracelet to some treasure from an antique shop.

LUCKY PERFUMES

The scents for Aquarians are jasmine, hyacinth, attar of roses and violet.

LUCKY FLOWERS AND TREES

Aquarians love trees and the tiny wild flowers of the woods and hedgerows—and especially lucky for them are the fragile wood anemone, periwinkles, forget-me-nots, and tulips.

Wood anemones have always been thought of as fairy flowers. They are a natural barometer, and curl up when evening—or rain—approaches. The petals really close up because fairies shelter inside the flower and pull the petals around them for protection. A wood anemone sewn on one's coat will protect the wearer from pestilence.

Periwinkles once had power against 'wykked spirytis', and were regarded as an emblem of friendship and immortality. If planted outside a garden gate, they were an invitation to step inside. From the red periwinkle comes the expression 'in the pink of condition'.

Forget-me-nots are said to have grown up spontaneously on the field after the Battle of Waterloo. The flowers were once prized as an antidote to a scorpion's sting.

Tulips also bring luck to an Aquarian. They are both sophisticated flowers and fairy flowers. In the days of chivalry (when everyone understood the language of flowers), a red tulip signified warm affection. But fairies used them as cradles to rock baby elves to sleep.

HERBS AND FOODS

Herbs that are particularly beneficial to Aquarians are southernwood, tansy, yarrow, comfrey, and vervain.

Southernwood has dozens of interesting properties. Pliny regarded it as an aphrodisiac. Others bound up wounds with it, or burnt it to repel serpents.

Tansy is excellent for driving away fleas and for procuring immortality. Tansy tisane was drunk to aid digestion, dispel rheumatism or soothe the nerves, while tansy leaves worn in the shoe will charm away ague. Tansy is one of the herbs that flavour the liqueur chartreuse.

Yarrow was once used to staunch wounds. It was the herb that sprang from rust scraped from Achilles' spear.

He wrapped the leaves round the wound he had unwittingly inflicted on Hercules' son. In France yarrow is called 'carpenters' wort' and prescribed to heal all wounds caused by carpenters' tools. The herb has other virtues. If tied to a cradle, the baby will be protected from witches; if strewn on the threshold, no demons will enter the house.

Comfrey was cultivated in medieval gardens because of its great reputation as 'knitbone' or 'boneset', its colloquial names. In particular, it healed wounds inflicted by swords, spears, scythes and sickles. Externally, the leaves were made into fomentations for sprains and bruises.

Vervain was an extraordinarily valuable plant. Guns rubbed with vervain ensured that bullets always hit their mark, but a soldier going into battle would escape from his enemies if he wore vervain in his pockets. It was used in charms and love philtres, and as an aphrodisiac—and vervain tisanes soothed the nerves, cured insomnia and gout, and dispelled fevers. The herb was also involved in solemn rites of expiation, and a chaplet of vervain was worn by Roman heralds when announcing war or peace. It was a herb no one cared to be without.

Aquarians can starve quite cheerfully—or enjoy gourmet food (if someone else will prepare it). But foods they should eat regularly include apples, figs, spinach, carrots, cucumbers, chestnuts, lentils, lettuce, cabbage, strawberries and coconut.

Coconut fudge or coconut chocolate would put a lovely 'full stop' to an Aquarian party if handed round with coffee—and a glass of chartreuse, the famous liqueur that tansy helps to flavour.

Pisces

The Fishes   21st February to 20th March

Giving a party for a Piscean?

Plan a buffet dinner party. In spite of their natural shyness, Pisceans are excellent guests with something to say to everyone, and their ready smile will warm the other guests' hearts. A buffet party will encourage them to circulate, and if there are several Pisceans there, they will probably all talk about how they were stage-struck at some time in their lives.

YOUR GUESTS

When entertaining your Piscean friend, invite some other Pisceans. They appreciate one another's wisdom and compassion. Also include some Leos (both signs bestow a histrionic ability), some Taureans and Librans who share the Piscean love of music, painting or literature, a few talented Scorpios, and some of the gifted, affectionate Cancerians.

LUCKY DAYS

Hold your party on the seventh or on a Thursday, the lucky Piscean days.

PISCEAN CHARACTERISTICS

Pisceans often hide their real feelings behind a smile, but look behind that smile and you will find qualities you will appreciate in any guest. They are loyal and generous, sensitive, understanding—tolerant of everyone's foibles, a little vague perhaps, but tender and loving, artistic, and with a gift for mimicry (if they can overcome their diffidence).

The sign of Pisces is fishes facing in opposite directions. This sometimes means that Piscean people like to be all things to all men, and agree too readily to other people's ideas and suggestions. You may not want to invite these Pisceans to your party, nor the ones who are self-indulgent, who forget to fulfil promises, who are moody, too apt to be clinging vines, and who waste their very considerable talents.

ICE-BREAKER

Piscean people have sudden hunches, so they will enjoy trying their luck with 'Divination by Dominoes'. To play this, remove the blanks from a domino set, and turn all the other pieces face downwards. Shuffle them, and let your guest choose three at random, while making a secret wish.

Here are the clues to the meaning of the pieces. With a little practice you will be able to string the clues together to make an entertaining interpretation for your guest's benefit.

One	and	One	A stranger from afar
One	and	Two	A pleasant journey
One	and	Three	A wish postponed
One	and	Four	Talk of money. A rise? A bonus?
One	and	Five	A new lover or a new job
One	and	Six	An engagement or a wedding
Two	and	Two	A wish fulfilled
Two	and	Three	Good prospects for a journey
Two	and	Four	Disappointment involving a friend

Two	and	Five	Luck at business
Two	and	Six	Good fortune surrounds you
Three	and	Three	You must wait a while
Three	and	Four	Don't listen to rumours
Three	and	Five	A happy reunion
Three	and	Six	News in a letter
Four	and	Four	A puzzle to be solved
Four	and	Five	Outing to the country— great fun!
Four	and	Six	Don't worry!
Five	and	Five	Paper work is important
Five	and	Six	You will need professional advice
Six	and	Six	Happiness for you and a loved one

LUCKY STONES

The stones to bring luck to Piscean people (whose planet is Jupiter) are amethyst, agates, emeralds and peridots.

Joseph and Mary are said to have been married with a ring set with an amethyst. The stone quickened wits, preserved soldiers in danger, and helped hunters capture wild animals. The power of an amethyst is even greater if it is engraved with a sun and moon.

Agates will bring peace of mind, reduce fevers, prevent a rider from being unhorsed, and cure poisoning.

Emeralds, like all green stones, were thought to be good for eyesight, and no spell could be cast on anyone wearing an emerald, which also brought happiness and domestic bliss.

Peridots were once called 'evening emeralds', as they were thought to be visible only after dark. If you own one, it will dispel anxieties of the night.

PRESENTS FOR PISCEANS

Pisceans need warm, comfortable and congenial surroundings, so presents that add a pleasant touch to their
homes will be appreciated—a beautiful table lamp, a per-
fumed candle, a lovely cup and saucer, a beautiful vase,
some caddies of tea (Pisceans are great tea drinkers), lacy
nighties, silky scarves, soft bedjackets, beautiful jewellery,
a delicate ornament, books (especially biographies), and
records of opera performances or symphony concerts.
They often like birthday presents and 'unbirthday'
presents more than Christmas presents. Perhaps it is their
romantic streak, for they will be more touched by a
bouquet of flowers on some anniversary than they will by
a present for a common-or-garden Christmas. Pisceans,
above all other people, appreciate hand-made presents,
even if made by unskilled childish fingers. Piscean men
also like tea—and antiques, books, gardening tools and
gardening gloves and seeds, and fishing rods.

(Piscean children are usually artistic, so any craft hobby
kit or a painting set would be an acceptable gift. Girls
would love an indoor garden—or a book of romances or
fairy tales. They are full of dreams!)

The lucky metal for Pisceans is tin. So, an assortment
of tea in decorative tins would make a very welcome gift.
Wrap them up and tie them up with mauve paper and
purple ribbon, the lucky colours for Pisceans, and give
them a lovely caddy spoon to go with the tea.

LUCKY PERFUMES

Pisceans love the rich perfume of wallflowers, cherry
blossom, Palma violet and lilac.

LUCKY FLOWERS AND TREES

Lucky trees for Pisceans are firs, mistletoe, rowans and
date palms.

A fir-tree is king of the forest. They were once considered lucky for newlyweds, who were given branches of fir with lighted candles affixed—like miniature Christmas trees.

Mistletoe has always been looked on as a magical plant, and, apart from its medicinal virtues, it brings good luck, has the strange power of opening all locks, while a sprig worn round the neck will keep witches at bay.

Rowan-trees are also magical. Sometimes sprigs are woven into thatches to keep the house safe from witches and bad fairies, and rowan branches hung over doors and stable gates will protect both man and beast.

Date palms for centuries have been regarded as something special. In the East it was believed that the trees possessed intelligence and were only one step removed from the animal kingdom. When Adam was driven out of Paradise he took three things with him, a root of myrtle, an ear of wheat—and a date.

Flowers that will bring luck to Pisceans are mauve crocuses, mauve orchids and foxgloves.

The ancient Romans had a great affection for crocuses. They strewed their apartments with the flowers, and drank crocus cordial to strengthen the heart, prevent disease and to arouse feelings of love. The Greeks wore garlands of crocuses at wedding festivals. The flowers were thought to ensure laughter and joy.

Mauve orchids were once regarded as aphrodisiacs, and it was believed that one of the favourite foods of the satyrs was orchid roots.

Foxgloves have always been linked with fairies. In Wales they are sometimes called 'goblins' gloves', and when a foxglove plant bends its stalk it is actually bending down to receive an elf who wants to rest within the safety of the bell.

HERBS AND FOODS

Among the herbs and spices specially beneficial to Pisceans are burnet, cumin and cinnamon.

Burnet was a useful plant to grow in any garden. Three stalks placed in a cup of wine would refresh the heart and dispel melancholy; burnet cordial was good for rheumatism; burnet juice would relieve toothache, and the fresh foliage was used to treat soldiers' wounds on the field of battle.

Cumin has been cultivated since before the birth of Christ. It was eaten as a stimulant, and planted with incantations to preserve one's well-being and to avert the Evil Eye. The seeds were baked in cakes to prevent their being stolen by demons—and country girls would try to persuade their lovers to eat cumin-seed cakes to ensure their fidelity.

Cinnamon was once the most distinguished of all the spices, and its history can be traced back to 5,000 B.C. At one time all love potions contained cinnamon. It was used in sacred rituals and ceremonies by Egyptians and Hebrews in their temples and tabernacles—and cinnamon is still one of the main ingredients in incense for churches.

Cinnamon was a costly spice. It had to be brought—by out-riggers or rafts without sails, oars or rudders—right across the oceans from the Far East to the Mediterranean, on journeys that sometimes took up to five years. The sailors and merchants told stories of cinnamon trees guarded by inaccessible cliffs, winged serpents and bats. Pliny the Elder, the inquisitive Roman, who spent his life collecting miscellaneous information, declared scornfully that the stories were 'all nonsense', and were invented to push up the price of cinnamon. But even after it was landed, it still had to be transported by mules, elephants,

horses, camels—and men. The Romans were willing to
pay handsomely for this warmly scented spice. They
believed it was beneficial to men's hearts.

For foods, give Pisceans apples and potatoes, walnuts,
almonds, strawberries, radishes, pumpkins, cucumbers,
spinach, beans, onions and barley. At the end of the
party, when you are serving coffee, hand round chocolate
almonds or sugared almonds, or walnut fudge—and for
a liqueur, offer your guests the cumin-flavoured crême de
menthe.

TAILPIECE

If you are in love with someone of the 'wrong' sign, don't worry. Marriages are made in heaven, not in the 'stars'.

BIBLIOGRAPHY

About Herbs; Dr Benedict Lust.
Are You Superstitious? Lorne Cowan.
The Book of Amber; George Williamson.
The Book of Days; published by Chambers.
A Book of Herbs; Dawn Macleod.
Brewer's Dictionary of Phrase and Fable.
Christmas and its Customs; Christina Hole.
Curious Lore of Precious Stones; G. F. Kunz.
*Demonology, Sympathetic Magic and
    Witchcraft;* J. N. Friend.
Encyclopaedia Britannica.
Encyclopaedia of Superstition; E. and M. Radford.
Endless Cavalcade; Alexander Howard.
The First of Trees; Robert Standish.
Flora and Folklore of Shakespeare; F. G. Savage.
Flora Symbolica; J. Ingram.
Flowers through the Ages; Gabriele Tergit.
Gem Stones; G. F. Herbert Smith.
A Herbal of All Sorts; Geoffrey Griggson.
Herbcraft; Violet Schafer.
Herbs; H. L. V. Fletcher.
Herbs and the Fragrant Garden; Margaret Brownlow.
Home Garden Book of Herbs and Spices;
    Milo Miloradovich.
Kitchen and Table; Colin Clair.
Language and Sentiments of Flowers; compiled and
    edited by L. V.
Leisure and Pleasure in Roman Egypt; Jack Lindsay.
Naming of Wild Flowers; Gareth H. Browning.

BIBLIOGRAPHY—*continued*

Of Herbs and Spices; Colin Clair.
Old English Customs and Ceremonies; Drake Carrell.
Plant Lore, Legends and Lyrics; R. Folkard.
Pleasures of Herbs; Aubrey Wynne Hatfield.
*Precious Stones—Their Occult Power and Hidden
    Significance;* W. B. Crow.
The Roman Cookery Book; translated by Barbara Flower
    and Elizabeth Rosenbaum.
Spice Trade of the Roman Empire—29 B.C.-A.D. 641;
    J. Innes Miller.
Standard Dictionary of Folklore.
The Story of Jewelry; M. Baerwald and J. Mahoney.
The Sun King; Nancy Mitford.
Traditions, Superstitions, etc.; C. Hardwick.
Wild Flowers of the Wayside and Woodlands; compiled
    by T. H. Scott and W. J. Stokoe.
Witches' Guide to Gardening; Dorothy Jacob.

INDEX

INDEX—*continued*